# REQUIEM FOR
# DEMOCRACY?

# REQUIEM FOR DEMOCRACY?

Lewis M. Andrews
Marvin Karlins

**Holt, Rinehart and Winston, Inc.**
NEW YORK   CHICAGO   SAN FRANCISCO   ATLANTA   DALLAS
MONTREAL   TORONTO   LONDON   SYDNEY

Copyright © 1971 by Holt, Rinehart and Winston, Inc.
All rights reserved
Library of Congress Catalog Card Number: 71-149092
**SBN: 03-078120-5 (Paper)**
**SBN: 03-085981-6 (Cloth)**
Printed in the United States of America
1   2   3   4       090       9   8   7   6   5   4   3   2   1

# ACKNOWLEDGMENTS

One of the real joys in writing this book was confronting colleague after colleague who enthusiastically and un selfishly contributed his efforts in our behalf. To everyone who contributed so mightily we gratefully record our gratitude:

Albert Bandura
Joseph Barmack
Julian Jaynes
Bertram Koslin
Thomas Kuhn
Joshua Lederberg
Seymour Levine
Gary Lynch
Joseph Notterman
David Rosenhan
Wallace Russell
Wilbur Schramm
Harold Schroder
James Voss

Although these men have made valuable contributions, we do not mean to imply that they necessarily share our views.

# CONTENTS

# REQUIEM FOR DEMOCRACY?

# 1 BRAVE NEW BEHAVIOR CONTROL: THE FINAL REVOLUTION?

*We have had religious revolutions, we have had political, industrial, economic, and nationalistic revolutions. All of them, as our descendants will discover, were but ripples in an ocean of conservatism—trivial by comparison with the psychological revolution toward which we are so rapidly moving. That will really be a revolution. When it is over, the human race will give no further trouble.*
Aldous Huxley

John Watson had a way with people. He was a flamboyant blend: a good measure of personal charisma spiced with a pinch of *chutzpuh* and a dash of brilliance. His dynamism vaulted Watson to the forefront of American psychology in the years surrounding World War I, when he founded Behaviorism.

John Watson also had a way with words. One of his much-quoted statements is of particular interest:

Give me a dozen healthy infants, well formed, and my own specified world to bring them up in and I'll guarantee to take any one at random and train him to become any type of specialist I might select—doctor, lawyer, artist, merchant-chief, and, yes, even beggar-man and thief, regardless of his talents, penchants, tendencies, abilities, vocations, and race of his ancestors (Watson, 1924).

As one might surmise, Watson was a firm advocate of human behavior control. He sincerely believed that such control was feasible and, unlike many of his contemporaries who speculated on such matters but went no further, he set out to substantiate his claims in the laboratory. His proof was gathered at the expense of Albert, a normal, healthy infant. Albert was basically stolid and unemotional. He cried infrequently, didn't scare easily and—except when confronted with loud sounds—showed no signs of fear. At nine months of age, he was suddenly presented with objects he had never seen before —including a white rat, rabbit, dog, monkey, cotton, and wool—and he approached these objects without apprehension.

At this juncture Watson set out to prove his point: that he could control Albert's behavior at will and, specifically, make him afraid of the white rat he now approached fearlessly. The animal was admitted into Albert's playroom as before, but now each time the child reached for the animal, a loud gong was struck nearby. After a very few of these encounters, Albert began to cry and scurry away whenever he saw the rat—even when the gong did *not* sound. Further, the child showed fear of other objects that looked like a rat, for example, the white rabbit he earlier approached without fear. By a few pairings of a negative reinforcer (loud sound) with an initially attractive plaything, Watson was effectively able to condition little Albert's behavior and make him afraid of a whole class of objects similar to, and including, a white rat.

Yet even with these experimental findings Watson was unable to convince many people of his beliefs. Who could take him seriously? After all, in the 1920s psychology was an infant science, recently born of philosophy. It had yet to prove itself. And despite Watson's boasts, the gap from limited experiments on animals and children (like little Albert) to comprehensive behavior control seemed infinite.

Things are different today. People's attitudes have changed. Consider, for example, these words:

> The time has come when if you give me any normal human being and a couple of weeks . . . I can change his behavior from what it is now to whatever you want it to be, if it's physically possible (McConnell, as quoted in Budrys, 1966).

This statement, remarkably similar to Watson's, was made in 1966 by James McConnell, a well-known contemporary psychologist. Today many people are willing to listen to McConnell's statement, and some even believe it. Why is McConnell noted when Watson was basically ignored? Because during the half century that separates the Watson and McConnell pronouncements, man has reached the threshold of controlling his own psychosocial evolution. Dramatic advances in all areas of behavioral science are converging to negate the long-held assumption that human behavior is somehow immune to scientific control.

In this first chapter of our book we will review some of these scientific advances in behavior control.

Many Americans find the idea of behavior control repugnant—the antithesis of the democratic ideal. Yet, need it be so? In 1948 Harvard psychologist B. F. Skinner published *Walden Two,* a novel about a scientifically regulated community. Skinner saw his scientifically shaped society as something befitting man's dignity—a place where a person could attain self-fulfillment and live joyously. How will behavior control techniques affect current American society? Will they provide us with a new sense of worth and freedom, or will they produce a "psytocracy" where man is enslaved by psychological manipulation, responding mechanically to the whims of a benign or despotic government? To answer these important questions we will first have to examine the present status of behavior control procedures and their impact on human conduct.

## Behavior Control Technology in Twentieth Century America

It often startles, and sometimes frightens, the reader of books like *Brave New World* and *1984* to be informed that the behavior control fantasies of a Huxley or Orwell are scientifically feasible procedures today. Professor Perry London of the University of Southern California puts it this way:

> As 1984 draws near, it appears that George Orwell's fears for Western democracy may have been too pessimistic, or at least premature, but it is also clear that his conceits of the technology by which tyranny could impress its will upon men's minds were much too modest. By that time, the means at hand will be more sophisticated and efficient than Orwell ever dreamed, and they will be in at least modest use, as they have already begun to be (London, 1969).

Confronted with London's statement, many people want to know what kinds of techniques have been developed that permit the control of human behavior. Surprisingly, perhaps, the currently most effective or promising approaches to regulating human conduct are not always the ones that have received widest public attention.

For example, most Americans are familiar with hypnosis and brainwashing as supposed behavior control procedures, but how many have heard of *electrical stimulation of the brain?* Those who are unacquainted with this procedure are unaware of a potentially powerful method of control.

Although work in brain stimulation is at least a century old, its possible value as a behavior control method was not recognized until the early 1950s, when a new Ph.D. named James Olds discovered the wellspring of Elysium in a most unexpected place.

Olds had wondered what would happen if he electrically stimulated the brain of a rat. To find out, he placed an elec-

trode inside the rodent's head and "turned on the juice" whenever the animal approached a designated spot on a large table.
How did the rat respond? Did it stay clear of the area where
the intercranial shock had been delivered (meaning the stimulation had been aversive) or approach the locale again (meaning the electric jolt had been rewarding)? Olds found that his
experimental subjects seemed to "get a charge" from the elec-
tricity. That is, they approached the area where they had received the electrical stimulation and centered their activities
around that spot.

To further clarify his rather unexpected findings Olds
conducted a series of experiments, the results of which pointed
to a series of "pleasure" and "pain" "centers" in the rat's
brain.[1] When the rat was electrically stimulated in a "pleasure
center," it performed acts aimed at reproducing the stimulation. Conversely, when it was stimulated in a "pain center," it
tried to avoid further stimulation. In the 15 or so years since
Olds' pioneer work the effects of brain stimulation found in
rats have been found in many other lower animals as well.

The most impressive aspect of brain stimulation is the
fact that animals low on the phylogenetic scale (such as cats or
rats) display rigid, stimulus-bound behavior in the face of it.
When one witnesses an animal under the influence of chemical or electrical stimulation of the brain he cannot help being
awed by how the organism's behavior can be turned "on" and
"off" at the experimenter's will. Another impressive aspect of
brain stimulation is what it can induce an animal to do or not
to do. For example, brain stimulation has been used to make
animals docile or savage, alert or lethargic, dominant or sub-
missive, and obese or emaciated. With brain stimulation rats
have been known to press a lever up to 7000 times an hour to
get an intercranial electric jolt; female animals have under-
taken male sexual behavior (one female rat tried to mount her
male partner unsuccessfully for eight weeks!); and male animals have developed an unquenchable sexual appetite (copu-
lating with their partners as long as stimulation continued).

As research has evolved, more and more behaviors of more and more animals under brain stimulation have been observed and reported. Some of the most interesting reports come from Yale physiologist José Delgado. In one of his more dramatic demonstrations of "electric power" Delgado staged an unusual bullfight, replacing the matador's skill with a device that could transmit signals to electrodes implanted in the bull's head. When the bull began to charge, the matador (Delgado himself) pushed a button on the transmitter, causing a shock in the bull's brain, whereupon the animal halted abruptly and lost interest in the matador. Delgado has also made mother monkeys, who are normally gentle and loving parents, savagely attack their offspring under the influence of electrical brain stimulation.

What of brain stimulation work with humans? Delgado has not ignored his fellow man! Reading his latest book, *Physical Control of the Mind,* one gets a feeling for the power and promise of brain implants as an instrument of behavior control. Delgado begins by stating that brain stimulation in man has "blocked the thinking process, inhibited speech and movement, or in other cases has evoked pleasure, laughter, friendliness, verbal output, hostility, fear, hallucinations, and memories." Then he describes some of the results he has obtained from human brain stimulation, results we summarize below:

> In one patient stimulation in the motor cortex section of the brain evoked a flexion of the right hand. Even at the doctor's request, the patient was unable to keep his fingers extended when stimulation was administered. Unable to control the fist-clenching response, the patient commented aptly: "I guess, Doctor, that your electricity is stronger than my will."

> Stimulation of the brain produced a state of fear in a female patient. Her fear, which lasted the duration of the electrical stimulation, was perceived as real and involved the belief that a horrible disaster was about to befall her.

> Assaultive behavior was elicited in a young female with a history of uncontrollable violent rage. Her electrically induced

fits of pique were similar to those she spontaneously experienced. One such stimulation occurred while the patient was happily playing a guitar. After a few seconds of the stimulation she hurled the guitar away and attacked a nearby wall.

Electrical stimulation of the brain produced pleasurable sensations in three epilepsy patients. One patient, a bright and attractive 30-year-old woman, experienced a pleasant feeling of relaxation when stimulated. Her talking increased, as did the intimacy of her subject matter. Her enjoyment must have been intense: normally reserved and poised, the patient ", , , openly expressed her fondness for the therapist (who was new to her), kissed his hands, and talked about her immense gratitude for what was being done for her."

A second female patient was not to be outdone. Reporting that she liked the stimulation "very much" and that it caused an "enjoyable tingling sensation in the left side of her body 'from my face down to the bottom of my legs'" the patient became increasingly talkative and flirtatious as stimulation continued; finally expressing her desire to marry the therapist!

Even a young male patient seemed emotionally attached to the doctor. After receiving several electrical stimulations which he fully enjoyed ("Hey!" he exclaimed, "you can keep me here longer when you give me these; I like those") he expressed a fondness for the male interviewer, one such expression accompanied by "a voluptuous stretch." Further stimulation got the patient talking about sexual activity. At one point he said, "I was thinkin' if I was a boy or a girl—which one I'd like to be." Following another stimulation he remarked with evident pleasure: "You're doin' it now," and then he said, "I'd like to be a girl."

Delgado is not alone in reporting rather dramatic behavior alterations as a function of brain stimulation. At Tulane Medical Center, for example, Dr. Robert Heath has published studies that lend further support to the hypothesis that pleasure centers exist in the brains of men as well as of rats!

In an experiment of particular interest, Heath implanted a series of electrodes into the brains of two patients.

The first patient, a 28-year-old man, suffered from narcolepsy, a condition that caused him to go from a state of total wakefulness to deep sleep in a matter of seconds. In an attempt to combat the narcolepsy, Heath outfitted the patient with a self-contained, transistorized brain stimulation unit that he could wear on his belt and operate by himself.

The stimulation unit had three buttons. Each one, when depressed, triggered an electrical stimulus in a different segment of the patient's brain. After pushing the various buttons several times, the patient reported he felt "good" when he depressed button one; "lousy" when he pushed button two; and "OK" when he held down the third button. From his button-pressing pattern it became obvious that button one "must be doing something right": the patient pressed it to the exclusion of buttons two and three. (The feeling aroused by button two was so distasteful that the patient placed a modified hairpin under the button so it could not be depressed.) When asked why he pushed button one so frequently, he replied that it gave him a good feeling—"as if he were building up to a sexual orgasm."

Button number one had a "bonus" value. The electrical stimulation it triggered did more than please the patient; it also alerted him, thereby giving him the means to fight his narcolepsy. Now each time he felt himself "going under" he pushed button one and literally jolted himself out of sleep.

Sometimes, when the narcoleptic state approached so suddenly that the patient didn't have time to press the button before he fell asleep, fellow patients and friends would arouse him by pushing the button for him. Because the patient could control his symptoms with the belt stimulator he was able to return part-time to his job as a nightclub entertainer.

Heath's second patient, a psychomotor epileptic with impulsive behavior problems, also tended to concentrate his self-stimulation activity on one button. This time, however, the button chosen delivered a stimulus that was irritating rather than pleasurable. When the patient was asked why he persisted in choosing the unpleasant stimulus, he explained that he wanted to bring into clearer focus a memory suggested by the stimulation.

The patient was also able to experience a pleasurable sensation by pressing a button triggering stimulation in the septal region of his brain. Upon experiencing this stimulation the patient often made verbal reference to sexual topics. When asked why he spoke of sexual subjects during the pleasurable stimulation he replied, "I don't know why that came to mind —I just happened to think of it." This finding—that pleasurable brain stimulation seems to be associated with a sexual motive state—is similar to results Delgado obtained with his three epileptic patients.

One of the most interesting aspects of the Heath study was the patient who attempted to bring an elusive memory to awareness by vigorously stimulating one section of his brain. One wonders if electrical stimulation of the brain might not be used to elicit the recall of memories in other men. Work conducted in Montreal by brain surgeon Wilder Penfield and his associates suggests it can be.

William James once used the term "stream of consciousness" to refer to one aspect of man's cognitive behavior. Penfield's description of his patients' cognitive behavior when they were electrically stimulated is in metaphorical harmony with James:

> There is an area of the surface of the human brain where local electrical stimulation can call back a sequence of past experience. . . . It is as though a wire recorder, or strip of cinematographic film with sound track, had been set in motion within the brain. The sights and sounds, and the thoughts, of a former day pass through the man's mind again (Penfield, 1959).

Dr. Penfield went fishing in the human stream of consciousness for memories—his fishing pole a thin wire, his hook an electrode, his bait an electrical stimulus. And he was successful. When he stimulated the cerebral cortex, his patients recalled moments from the past. What they recalled was not very significant (one young boy heard his mother on the phone) but so vivid that they had difficulty believing the event wasn't actually taking place. One woman who heard an orchestra playing every time the electrode was activated "believed that a gramophone was being turned on in the operating room on each occasion, and she asserted her belief stoutly in a conversation some days after the operation" (Penfield, 1959). Another patient, a male, clearly heard his cousins laughing—a somewhat disquieting experience since his cousins were in South Africa and he was on an operating table in Canada.

The idea of electric memory retrieval has fascinated many contemporary writers. Author and scientist Arthur C. Clark has suggested an interesting application for such a procedure. People who reach old age and have no interest in the future may have an opportunity to relive the past and to create again those they knew and loved when younger. "Even this . . . might not be a preparation for death, but the prelude to a new birth" (Clark, 1963). Even more provocative is Clark's suggestion that artificial memories could be composed, taped, and then fed into the brain by electrical or other means. This ultimate form of entertainment has been imagined in D. C. Compton's novel *Synthajoy*.

Where will the research of men like Delgado, Heath, and Penfield eventually take us? When it comes to assessing the future of brain stimulation as a behavior control device, there is no dearth of commentators. Science writer Albert Rosenfeld provides this scenario:

> One can easily imagine people in the future wearing self-stimulating electrodes (it might even become the "in" thing to do) which might render the wearer sexually potent at any time; that might put him to sleep or keep him awake, according to

his need; that might curb his appetite if he wanted to lose weight; that might relieve him of pain; that might give him courage when he was fearful, or render him tranquil when he was enraged (Rosenfeld, 1969).

As one might suspect, some people are openly dismayed about the prospects for brain stimulation. Delgado's work, for example, has been sufficiently alarming to arouse press commentary. On April 10, 1967, the *New York Times* published the following editorial entitled "Push-Button People?"

There are disquieting implications in the experiments on control of human beings and animals that Prof. José M. R. Delgado of Yale Medical School has successfully conducted. His latest feat has been to demonstrate that by implanting electordes in a female monkey's brain he can make it reject its own child on radio command. Two years ago he revealed that he had been able to stop a charging bull in mid-course and make it amble obediently away in response to the same type of electronic stimulation.

It is the possibility of similar control over human beings that causes concern. Several years ago Dr. Delgado told a scientific meeting that experiments with patients suffering from epilepsy or emotional illness seem to "support the distasteful conclusion that motion, emotion, and behavior can be directed by electrical forces and that humans can be controlled like robots by push buttons." It is indeed a "distasteful conclusion" despite Dr. Delgado's assurance that electrical stimulation "cannot change the basic characteristics of the experimental subject."

It is quite conceivable that in some countries investigations may be under way into the possibility of using these techniques to control human beings. Presumably there is still a long way to go before Dr. Delgado's accomplishments with monkeys can be successfully transferred to humans. But the mere existence of such a possibility is disturbing, and certainly merits wider public discussion and greater attention than it has received up to now.[2]

Is the *Times*'s concern with brain stimulation justified? Might man ever be controlled by intercranial electrical inputs —attached to electrodes and wires like a puppet on strings? Delgado thinks not.

> Fortunately [he claims], the prospect is remote, if not impossible, not only for obvious ethical reasons, but also because of its impracticability. . . . This technique requires specialized knowledge, refined skills, and a detailed and complex exploration in each individual. . . . The application of intracerebral electrodes in man will probably remain highly individualized and restricted to medical practice.

Yet one wonders if Delgado's assurances are not a bit premature. Of course, with our present knowledge it would be impossible to implement control by brain stimulation on a mass scale. But what about 20 years from now? Or 50? Why shouldn't brain stimulation be an effective behavior control procedure in, say, 2070? Certainly technology shouldn't be a stumbling block. Already in Delgado's own laboratory patients sport long-lasting implanted electrodes that can be hidden under wigs and activated by remote control. With steady improvements in micro-miniaturization and complex circuitry, the limits of brain stimulation technology stop only at the boundaries of the scientist's imagination.

But if, as it seems, technology won't present a barrier to development of a brain stimulation system of behavior regulation, it is still possible that brain stimulation will prove insufficient as a means of controlling human conduct. On the basis of current research findings, this is a reasonable doubt to entertain. Thus far there is a major difference between human and rat behavior under the influence of brain stimulation: unlike lower animals, who display rigid, stimulus-bound behavior in the face of brain stimulation, man seems quite able to control his own actions while undergoing such treatment. Whereas under the electrical probe animals become electrified automatons, man retains his autonomy.

Will man ever be as subject to regulation by brain stimulation as his furry relatives? One cannot yet be sure. Due to obvious ethical considerations, brain stimulation work with humans is just beginning. Until further research is conducted the ultimate promise and power of this control technique must remain in doubt. But from knowledge of comparative physiology, one speculative observation does seem in order. The brain structures underlying emotive behavior are basically the same in lower animals and man. The similarity of these "primitive" brain structures in lower and higher organisms makes one suspect that man's emotional behavior might be more open to regulation by brain stimulation than is his intellective functioning, which is controlled by a section of the brain unique to the human species.

Brain stimulation is but one mode of behavioral control. *Behavior modification* is another. Like brain stimulation, it is not among the most highly publicized control techniques; unlike brain stimulation, it functions upon the organism externally rather than internally.

Behavior modification is a scientific procedure for systematically changing behavior through the use of rewards or punishments, or both. Defined in such a manner, free of scientific jargon, the method seems, to some people, to offer nothing new. In one way these people are correct: the man who purchases flowers for his wife or spanks his child is practicing a rudimentary form of behavior modification ("rudimentary" in comparison to the more sophisticated, more effective behavior modification used by scientists). On the other hand, these people are incorrect in assuming that behavior modification is "old hat." What makes the approach novel is the use of psychological learning principles in the reinforcement of behavior.

Although the major thrust of behavior modification is a product of the last 15 years, the impetus for the movement came from investigations in the earlier decades of this century.

One such study we have already described: Watson's experiment using loud sound to make little Albert afraid of a white rat. A second study, by Paul Fuller in 1949, reports an attempt to teach a "vegetative human organism" a simple response. As reported in the *American Journal of Psychology,* Fuller worked with an institutionalized 18-year-old patient who could neither walk nor talk. Day after day he lay flat on his back, unable to turn over, unable even to chew his food. According to hospital personnel, the patient had never learned to perform the simplest of tasks. Fuller set out to see if the young man could learn to raise his right arm to receive food. First, the patient was deprived of food for 15 hours; then, whenever he raised his right arm, he was syringe-fed a sugar-milk solution. After a few sessions the patient was raising his right hand regularly to receive a food reward. When the food was taken away, the hand-raising response "extinguished" (gradually disappeared in the absence of reinforcement).

The Watson and Fuller experiments share one important characteristic: the use of reinforcement to change behavior. Behavior modification works by increasing or decreasing the likelihood of a specified behavioral response through systematic reward and punishment. Little Albert received negative reinforcement (loud sound), and it is assumed that such punishment should eventually lead to cessation of the negatively reinforced behavior. In the case of the bedridden patient, the reinforcement was positive (food), and it is expected that rewarded behavior will be maintained (and often will increase in frequency). The process by which reinforcement becomes associated with certain behaviors is called conditioning. The scientist uses his knowledge of conditioning principles to make his efforts more effective.

One can get a feeling for the power of conditioning procedures—how such methods can systematically change a wide variety of human actions—by reading B. F. Skinner's novel. Although it is labeled a work of fiction, *Walden Two* is grounded in scientific facts, using the established learning principles underlying behavior modification to regulate human behavior and create a Utopian community. In reality, the book is a reflection of Skinner's scientific thinking from start to finish—an application of his operant conditioning methods to design a society created and governed by psychologists.

In *Walden Two,* every person is well behaved, happy, and productive. Citizens are controlled, but they are not aware of being controlled. Control is achieved by procedures similar to those employed by Watson with little Albert and by Fuller with the vegetative patient. Explains the novel's psychologist-hero:

> When he behaves as we want him to behave, we simply create a situation he likes, or remove one he doesn't like. As a result, the probability that he will behave that way again goes up, which is what we want. Technically it's called "positive reinforcement" (Skinner, 1948)

*Walden Two* is deeply grounded in the principles of behavior modification.

In the years since the early work of Skinner, Watson, and Fuller, scientists have made behavior modification a far more powerful system for controlling behavior. At the same time they have used it to change increasingly complex and diverse types of human activity. A large proportion of current behavior modification takes place in clinical settings, where it is used to eliminate or modify dysfunctional personal behavior. The ability of behavior modification to change entrenched, highly resistant forms of human activity reminds us of its potency as a behavior control device.

Consider, for example, the work described by A. B. Goorney a specialist in neuropsychiatry at the R.A.F. Hospital in Wroughton, England. Dr. Goorney used behavior modification to treat a highly complex adult behavior: compulsive gambling. His patient was a 37-year-old man who had been playing the horses for 13 years. Unhappy at home and unlucky at the track, this gambler faced a dissolving marriage and a depleted bankroll. It was, in fact, the wife who referred the man for therapy, concerned that his continuing losses would bring financial ruin.

To treat the gambler required, first, a full understanding of his problem. This was accomplished through interviews between Dr. Goorney and the patient. Discussion revealed a man who began gambling shortly after the start of a disappointing marriage—a compulsive bettor who wagered until his funds evaporated (he always lost) or his wife intervened. During gambling bouts the patient spent most of his waking hours thinking about the horses. Mornings were spent picking selections from the racing forms, afternoons daydreaming about winning, and evenings anxiously listening to broadcast results of the races.

Once apprised of the patient's gambling pattern, Dr. Goorney was able to proceed with behavior modification therapy. The treatment chosen was negative reinforcement: a total of 675 brief but unpleasant electric shocks administered to the patient's upper arms during nine days of therapy. Each treatment day consisted of six 10-minute shock sessions, each session occurring during a time when the patient was involved in some phase of his gambling pattern (for example, studying the racing form). The strategy behind this approach was straightforward: to cure the patient of his compulsion, it was necessary to treat *all* behaviors related to gambling.

The results of this aversive reinforcement were shocking, to say the least! Halfway through therapy the patient indicated a decreasing interest in some of the activities related to his habit; by the seventh treatment day he was essentially cured, showing no desire to even hear the results of the races. One month after therapy had been terminated the patient claimed that all interest in horseracing had disappeared and that harmony was beginning to appear in his marriage. A follow-up one year later found the patient reporting a continued lack of interest in horseracing and maintained progress in the marital situation.

Here then is an amazing therapeutic triumph. In the space of nine days a compulsive gambling habit of 13 years' duration is broken. Such is the power of behavior modification when it is skillfully used to control the actions of man.[3] Another example of behavior modification in a therapeutic setting is contained in Gerald Davison's 1968 case report of a 21-year-old unmarried college senior with a sexual problem.

The troubled student, "Mr. M.," was initially referred to Dr. Davison by the University Counseling Center. A self-diagnosed sadist, the young man achieved sexual arousal through fantasies involving the torture of women. No sexual arousal was possible without the fantasies. Sadistic thoughts accompanying masturbation provided Mr. M. with his only sexual gratification. Concern over his condition had led him to severely limit his heterosexual contacts, and he firmly believed that marriage was impossible.

This would be no easy case! For 10 years Mr. M. had coupled sadistic fantasies with masturbation to attain his only satisfactory sexual fulfillment. How could the pattern be altered? Possibly by associating the pleasurable feelings of orgasm with something different from the customary reveries of torture. What if, for example, Mr. M. were asked to concentrate on a pin-up photo just before orgasm—to forget his fantasy and keep his mind on the picture. If the female form could replace the sadistic fantasy as the image associated with the intensely rewarding sexual response, attraction to women might be substituted for the desire to torture them.

Such a plan seemed worth a try. Mr. M. was instructed to continue masturbating, using sadistic fantasies to "start things off." Once an erection was achieved, however, a modification in procedure was recommended. Dr. Davison describes it this way:

He was then to begin to masturbate while looking at a picture of a sexy, nude woman; *Playboy* magazine was suggested to him as a good source. If he began losing the erection, he was to switch back to his sadistic fantasy until he could begin masturbating effectively again. Concentrating again on the *Playboy* picture, he was to continue masturbating, using the fantasy only to regain erection. As orgasm was approaching he was at all costs to focus on the *Playboy* picture, even if sadistic fantasies began to intrude. It was impressed on him that gains would ensue only when sexual arousal was associated with the picture, and that he need not worry about indulging in sadistic fantasies at this point. The client appeared enthusiastic and hopeful as he left the office (Davison, 1968).

Such optimism was not in vain. On his next visit to Davison's office the young man reported that *Playboy* had aided him in achieving successful orgasms without the sadistic fantasies. At this point Dr. Davison made suggestions geared to further therapeutic progress, encouraging Mr. M. to begin dating on a casual basis and, when masturbating, to try to achieve orgasm with the use of "real-life" pictures of women and imagined images of *Playboy* pin-ups. Efforts to carry out Dr. Davison's recommendations were not totally successful. During the third therapy session Mr. M. reported difficulty in making dates and ridding himself of his sadistic fantasies. This prompted Dr. Davison to take an additional therapeutic measure. He asked Mr. M. to imagine, for 5 minutes, a typical sadistic fantasy in conjunction with various repugnant images (for example, being kicked in the groin by a karate expert). Upon completing this unpleasant task, the patient was sent away for another week with instructions to continue masturbating, if possible, without the use of sadistic fantasies.

In the final three therapy sessions Mr. M. made steady progress toward the therapeutic goal: sexual arousal through "normal" procedures. The fourth session was marked by reports of successful masturbation to imagined images of women without appeal to dreams of torture, and the fifth session by

Mr. M.'s stated *inability* to obtain an erection to a sadistic fantasy. The patient praised the effectiveness of the therapy and told Dr. Davison about the satisfactions he had achieved through his newly initiated dating encounters. In the sixth session (one month later) Mr. M.'s dating efforts had decreased, but he claimed a continued absence of sadistic fantasies and the ability to masturbate successfully "to both real life and imaginal appropriate sexual stimuli."

Sixteen months after the termination of therapy a follow-up report was obtained. Except for a period of "premeditated" return to sadistic fantasies, Mr. M. seemed on the way to leading a normal social life, free of the sadism and loneliness he had known for a decade. In the patient's own words:

> I have no need for sadistic fantasies. . . . I have also been pursuing a vigorous (well, vigorous for *me*) program of dating. In this way, I have gotten to know a lot of girls of whose existence I was previously only peripherally aware As you probably know, I was very shy with girls before; well, now I am not one-fifth as shy as I used to be. In fact, by my old standards, I have become a regular rake! (Davison, 1968).

Fantastic? In many ways, yes. But as behavior modification techniques continue to develop and more qualified professionals use them to treat behavior disorders, findings like Davison's might well become commonplace. Already behavior modification has been used to solve a wide range of problems, and one suspects the possibility of an even greater range of applications in the near future. Some of these applications are just now being anticipated.

Consider behavior modification in the classroom. Might it be used to aid learning and regulate classroom behavior? Current research suggests it can. A team of investigators headed by Robert Hamblin (a professor of sociology at Washington University) has implemented a "token-exchange system" to calm aggressive children, to train two-year-olds to read as well as their five-year-old classmates; to encourage shy ghetto children to become above-average talkers; and to start autistic youths on the road to recovery. In a recent article, these scientists report that children (in good capitalistic fashion) will perform specific behaviors to "earn" tokens that they can exchange for valued prizes: Playdoh, movie admissions, snacks, and so forth. The teacher, by controlling the tokens, controls the behavior of the class. Reading Hamblin's report, one is amazed at how quickly and efficiently the teacher is able to produce the results he desires.

Consider, for example, token reinforcement in calming aggressive behavior. For this phase of their research the Hamblin team assembled a teacher's nightmare: a group of four-year-old boys so aggressive that psychiatrists and social workers had failed to tame them. An instructor was then asked to use her previous training and experience in teaching the five boys, that is, to fulfill the role of "typical teacher" using "typical educational procedures" in the classroom. The poor woman tried every tactic in her repertoire to no avail: after eight days of nerve-rattling effort she was stymied by children who committed an average of 150 aggressive acts per day!

At this point the hapless teacher was told of behavior modification techniques and instructed to (1) ignore aggression when possible (turn her back when it occurred) and (2) to reinforce, with tokens, any child who performed an act of cooperation. By the end of the experiment the boys' behavior had undergone marked change: cooperative acts had increased from approximately 55 to 180 per day while aggressive sequences plummeted from roughly 150 to 10! The authors comment:

> In "normal" nursery schools, our observations have shown that five boys can be expected to have 15 aggression sequences and 60 cooperation sequences per day. Thus, from extremely aggressive and uncooperative, our boys had become less aggressive and far more cooperative than "normal" boys (Hamblin et al., 1969).

The token exchange system has been used in mental institutions as well as classrooms. In general, behavior modification is being employed with increasing frequency with the mentally ill and retarded. One such application is presented by James Lent in his discussion of Mimosa Cottage, where behavior modification is used to train mentally retarded females to become functioning members of society. The therapy does not cure retardation, but it does provide the means for motivating the patients to learn the skills necessary to leave the hospital and live in the community The goal of Lent's work is to teach Mimosa girls behaviors expected of normally functioning individuals. This is done by teaching them skills most people take for granted: physical cleanliness, proper dress and grooming, correct posture and verbal behavior. All this is accomplished by reinforcing desired behavior with tokens—rewards that can be "cashed in" for items at the Cottage store or for trips into town. Speaking of several girls who have been successfully trained by the reinforcement procedure and have left Mimosa Cottage to live in the community, Lent concludes:

> They are not fully independent, but they are able to take care of most of their personal needs and to move about the community alone. . . . All of them lead simple but productive lives. Those around them may even forget, at times, that they were ever labeled "mentally retarded" (Lent, 1968).

Compulsive gambling. Sadistic fantasies. Aggressive behavior in the classroom. Improper social conduct. All complex behaviors controlled through behavior modification. One dramatic aspect of this behavior control procedure is its ability to change a person's conduct without his awareness that a change is taking place. A case in point concerns a psychologist and 17 students. The students were told to reinforce any statement made to them by friends and relatives that began with an expression of personal conviction: "I think," "I believe," "It

seems to me," or "I feel." They did this by smiling or para-
phrasing the statement in an agreeable fashion. In every case,
the friend or relative increased the rate at which he stated personal convictions. *In no case were the friends or relatives
aware that they were being conditioned.* The psychologist had
the additional shock of discovering that he himself was being
conditioned by a colleague to whom he was describing the results of his work! (Mann, 1965.)

Speculation on the future of behavior modification is
somewhat frightening to those who fear behavior control—
because all signs indicate that behavior modification will become an even more powerful tool for regulating human conduct in the coming years. *The power of reinforcement to
modify human behavior is one of the most pervasive and documented findings in modern psychology; and behavior modification is the first truly effective system to harness the power of
reinforcement in regulating man's actions.* In some ways it is
strange that scientists didn't hit upon behavior modification
earlier—after all, the principles upon which it is based are op-
erative all around us (just consider what people will do for
money!). Perhaps it is a case of the fish being the last organism to discover water.

Developments in behavior modification represent a dramatic advance in the technology of behavior control. Developments in the technology of *monitoring devices* represent
another advance, providing modern man with vastly improved
ways to amass and to utilize information about others in regulating their actions.

The importance of such information has long been recognized. Throughout history men have used knowledge of
other men to control behavior. Sometimes this control is obvious, as when a blackmailer uses information about a person
to extract payment or services; at other times, it is not so obvious, as when a poker player watches his opponent's facial expression for a possible tip-off on the cards he is holding. What

makes the control of behavior through knowledge of others different today is the sophistication of the monitoring devices used to collect information. In previous centuries information was gathered by word of mouth, keyhole visitations, intercepted letters, and a good deal of old-fashioned footwork. Now it is accumulated by the use of tape recorders, cameras, wiretapping, and radar. The old hotel detective has been replaced by girls with "bugs" in their bras, microphones in their martinis, and cameras in their cosmetic cases. Even James Bond is threatened with replacement by an orbiting spy satellite. In short, contemporary information-gathering procedures have evolved from the eye-and-ear stage to the era of electronic eavesdropping. Modern technology has expanded the reach and sensitivity of man's senses and, in so doing, has vastly improved his powers of surveillance. It has long been recognized that what a man says could be held against him; today we have the means to know what each man says—means far more powerful than Orwell's "telescreen." [4]

What conditions have brought about the dramatic advances in monitoring devices? There are several relevant factors, for instance the micro-miniaturization of information-gathering instruments. With the development of solid-state circuitry came the means for building reliable, powerful surveillance units and photographic equipment miniscule in size. Yet the most important single factor in creating sophisticated monitoring devices was the development of the computer.

With the computer man has produced an instrument capable of recording, storing, and quickly retrieving a plethora of information on each American citizen. Never before has any system or machine been available that could give man access to such increasingly refined and extensive data on 200 million people. The computer has made it possible to keep an up-to-date life history of every man, woman, and child in this country.

The implications of a computer-centered information-gathering system are just beginning to be appreciated.[5] With the computer, man is never free from his past; events of 20 years ago are remembered as well as yesterday's happenings by a machine with a perfect memory. The computer can be programmed to detect a dishonest taxpayer, trace a missing person, choose a spouse, pay a bill, and give medical advice. It can also determine a person's credit rating and current financial status.

There is currently talk of developing a national data bank for the purpose of getting each citizen "on tape" and into the computer. Already in one European country new babies are assigned a computer number for life. In America the venerated social security number could serve much the same purpose.

As more and more facts about more and more Americans become more and more available through the blessings of computer technology, we must assume that those who have access to such machines will also have access to information in a form best suited to control individual conduct. Most computer companies have denied the possibility of control, mostly for the sake of good public relations. But Robert P. Henderson, general manager of Honeywell's Electronic Data Processing Division, concedes that computers have potentially dangerous "side effects." He warns of information abuse and "pollution to privacy" (Allen, 1970). Such is the curse and the promise of our information-processing age.

Recent innovations in monitoring devices are promising to turn a hit-and-miss form of behavior control—surveillance—into a highly effective regulatory procedure. The same can be said for discoveries in another form of behavior control: *genetic engineering.*

There are two major forms of genetic engineering: selective breeding and genetic surgery. Advocates of selective breeding have been around a long time. Utopian theorists, such as Thomas More, as well as fascist fanatics, have recommended such a procedure to improve the human species. In 548 B.C. Theognis of Megara wrote:

One would not dream of buying cattle without thoroughly examining them, or a horse without knowing whether he came of a good stock; yet we see an excellent citizen being given to wife some wretched woman, daughter of a worthless father. . . . Fortune mixes the races, and the odious adulteration is bastardizing the species (Rostand, 1959).

A century later, Plato, in the *Republic,* advocated selective breeding. In order to make marriages as healthy as possible for the welfare of the state, he proposed adopting practices followed by breeders of dogs and birds of prey.

Today the technology of selective breeding is far more developed than it was in Plato's time, owing in large measure to the creation of a technique for efficiently freezing spermatozoa, thus making possible a greater frequency of successful conceptions than with artificial insemination of the usual type or even with natural insemination. Frozen sperm banks exist in the United States today, and their stocks can be expected to contribute to the more than 10,000 babies born every year in this country by means of artificial insemination.

A Nobel Prize-winning biologist, the late Dr. Herman J. Muller of Indiana University, has seen the frozen sperm banks as a way to avoid the difficulties and social mistakes of "old-style" eugenics movements.

The banks of germinal material that will thereby become available will include material derived from persons of outstanding gifts, intelligence, moral fiber, and physical fitness. In this way couples desiring to have in their own families one or more children who are especially likely to embody their own ideals of worth will be afforded a wide range of choice. They will be assisted by records of the lives and characteristics of the donors and of their relatives, and by counsel from diverse specialists, but the final choices will be their own and their participation will be entirely voluntary. It is to be expected that the use of this method will increase in the course of coming generations and will implement, on the genetic

side, a great advance in human brotherhood, intelligence, and
bodily vigor (Muller, 1965).

Frozen sperm banks—an important breakthrough in the science of selective breeding. And there are other, even more spectacular breakthroughs on the horizons. Like *artificial inovulation,* the process whereby a fertilized egg would be taken from the body of a donor woman and implanted in the womb of a prospective "mother" to grow and develop. Or *ectogenesis,* the development of test-tube babies—children created outside a womb altogether (à la *Brave New World*). Or even *cloning,* the procedure whereby biological "carbon copies" of a single individual could be produced by genetic manipulation. With all these revolutionary advances in the offing it is little wonder that the distinguished geneticist, Dr. Salvador Luria, has recommended that the United Nations, as well as the National Academy of Sciences, establish a committee to discuss the planned evolution of mankind (Luria, 1965).

Selective breeding presents a currently operational form of genetic engineering. Genetic surgery, on the other hand, is still on the drawing boards, where most people figured it would stay before the discovery of DNA, the chemical code for the genes. Then came the isolation and pictorial record of an actual gene—and almost overnight the goal of modifying the genetic code seemed in reach.

Since the discovery of DNA, scientists have been working on ways to preprogram children by chemically altering the DNA in newly formed embryos. This is a very difficult task because the DNA structure is complex and each body cell contains 46 chromosomes, or clusters of DNA strands. Nonetheless, Dr. Waclaw Szybalski, of the University of Wisconsin, has already succeeded in achieving transfers of chromosomes in laboratory samples of mammalian cells (Muller, 1965). Other biologists are trying to develop viruses or bacteria that can invade a human cell and alter a portion of DNA without damaging the cell.

Once we have mastered "genetic surgery" the opportunities for human control are practically unlimited. Dr. Kimball Atwood, of the University of Illinois, suggests that we could "produce an organism that combines the happy qualities of animals and plants, such as one with a large brain so that it can indulge in philosophy and also a photosynthetic area on its back so that it would not have to eat" (Atwood, 1965). Although we are still a good distance from creating the "Aniveg" envisioned by Professor Atwood, the first steps toward using genetic surgery to control behavior have been taken.

Developments in brain stimulation, behavior modification, monitoring devices, and genetic engineering represent impressive advances in the technology of behavior control. However, most of the interest in behavior control focuses on *drugs,* primarily because of the ease with which they can be used.

It will come as no shock to Americans to be told they live in a drug era. Some call it a psychedelic revolution. Grass. Hash. Dex. LSD. STP. The vocabulary of our turned-on, tripped-out generation. This is the golden age of pharmacology, the time of the tranquilizer, the marijuana moment. These are the decades when "Triple A" refers not to a motorists' association, but to Anacin, Alcohol, and Acid, when schools are first-rate drugstores, when a dislodged Harvard professor can start a religion that worships an illegal drug.

Possibly the popularity of drugs is explained by their undisputed power to affect the mind. Any person who has taken a stiff drink, sleeping compound, tranquilizer, or stimulant has experienced this power. So has the individual who uses drugs as a vehicle to explore that most personal and alluring frontier, the boundaries of his own psyche. What startles scientist and layman alike is the burgeoning number of drugs that have recently been developed to assault the human brain. In 1966, Dr. Stanley Yolles, Director of the National Institute of Mental Health, predicted before a Senate subcommittee: "The next five to ten years . . . will see a hundredfold increase in the number and types of drugs capable of affecting the mind."

As mind-influencing drugs increase in number, they cannot help but contribute to the control of ever greater amounts of human behavior. Already, drugs have demonstrated a remarkable effectiveness in regulating people's actions. In 1952, chlorpromazine, the first modern tranquilizing drug, entered the American market. Its immediate effect was enormous: it allowed treatment of "incurable" mental patients and superseded most forms of psychiatric surgery (for example, lobotomies). The impact of tranquilizing drugs in American mental institutions is well described by Dr. H. Himwich:

> The new tranquilizing drugs have introduced a new regime in the management of patients in mental hospitals. The drugs calm the patients without putting them to sleep. Their effects last longer than sedatives. They make it possible to keep severely disturbed patients in an open ward instead of locking them up. And, most important, they make even "hopeless" patients accessible to psychotherapy by reducing their anxiety and removing some of the barriers between the patient and the psychiatrist (Himwich, 1955).

The popularity of tranquilizers is not confined to the mental hospital. In 1960, tranquilizers were the third most common class of drugs dispensed by general practitioners, appearing in more than 10 percent of all prescriptions. By 1965, over 150 million prescriptions for mood-changing drugs were being filled annually, and it is estimated that in 1970 one in four American adults will use these drugs.

Major tranquilizers (effective in controlling the symptoms of schizophrenia and other psychotic states) are not the only psychopharmacological drugs that have been developed for common use within the past two decades. There are also the minor tranquilizers and sedatives, effective in relieving neurotic anxiety; stimulative drugs, used to decrease fatigue or to produce a euphoric feeling; and antidepressive drugs, used to relieve symptoms of depression.

In addition to psychopharmacological agents, "hormone

drugs" are also important in controlling human behavior. In recent times scientists have learned that genes accomplish their grand design by manufacturing chemicals called hormones, which regulate the growth of the body and supervise its day-to-day activities. Much of modern drug research is now dedicated to developing chemicals that do not alter the genes themselves but that suppress or replace various hormones. Glutamic acid has been used successfully in the experimental treatment and prevention of mongolism. Iodine is used to treat cretinism. Dr. Choh Hao Li, director of the Hormone Research Center in San Francisco, is synthesizing pituitary peptide, a growth hormone, for use in preventing dwarfism.

More dramatic experiments on laboratory animals indicate the potential power of hormone control. Hormone injections have been used to regulate basic drives, such as hunger and thirst, in rats. They have also been used to facilitate and to inhibit animal learning and to arouse fear, anxiety, and frustration. In a report submitted to the National Commission on the Causes and Prevention of Violence, Stanford biomedical researchers Seymour Levine and Robert Conner revealed results of an experiment that showed that the amount of aggression exhibited by animals is related to the amount of sex hormone in the bloodstream. Furthermore, male sex hormones produced a different style of fighting than female sex hormones (Levine & Conner, 1969). A Berkeley researcher predicts that we will soon have an anti-aggression pill that will reduce aggressive tendencies by neutralizing sex hormones in critical areas of the brain. A learning pill is also forecast. And, of course, the birth control pill—with all its social ramifications—is already here.

It seems that each new year brings with it new drugs for controlling behavior. Most of these potions are still medicinal in nature; yet in an article entitled "The Psychopharmacological Revolution," Murray Jarvik notes:

> One can envision the day when drugs may be employed not only to treat pathological conditions (reduce pain, suffering,

agitation, and anxiety), but also to enhance the normal state of man—increase pleasure, facilitate learning and memory, reduce jealousy and aggressiveness (Jarvik, 1967).

By learning more about the metabolism of the brain, the way LSD and other hallucinogens affect the mind,[6] and the chemical bases of intellective and emotive functioning, the contemporary scientist is doing everything necessary to make that day a reality.

Thus far we have considered the various behavior control methods independently of each other, but there is no reason why any of them must be used alone. To the contrary, such methods are maximally effective when used in combination. Consider the frequent inability of behavior modification to provide truly reinforcing reinforcements—reinforcements a person really desires or despises. Yet only when rewards and punishments are sufficiently attractive or repulsive will a person find it "worthwhile" to change his behavior. With advances in brain stimulation and psychopharmacology the possibility of developing effective reinforcements is enhanced. An individual who might be unwilling to modify his behavior for a cookie or a quarter might readily change if the payoff were a drug that provides an intensely pleasurable sensation.

One scholar has pondered what would happen if behavior modification, monitoring devices, and brain stimulation were combined into one integrated control procedure. He produces this intriguing speculation:

> If, for instance, a human subject had electrodes implanted in such a way that any ongoing action could be rewarded, punished, or prevented, and if micro-transmitters and receivers made external wires and apparatus unnecessary, he could be placed in a learning situation, and selected patterns of behavior could be encouraged or discouraged automatically. With effective monitoring and computing equipment, much of the process could be controlled automatically (Quarton, 1967).

The situation Quarton envisages has not yet taken place. However, the principle it illustrates has already been recognized: by combining behavior control procedures a system is created that is more powerful than any of its component parts operating alone. Such systems are being developed today for a more powerful behavior control technology tomorrow.

## Tho Future of Scientific Behavior Control

Perhaps the most astounding aspect of scientific behavior control is not what has been accomplished thus far but what seems likely to be accomplished in the near future. Scientific progress is like an avalanche: it builds on itself, expands, gains momentum, and increases in power. There is no reason to assume that scientific progress in human behavior control will slow or halt. To the contrary, it will probably increase in tempo, and as long as it does we can be quite sure that the effectiveness of behavior control techniques will be enhanced. *How effective* they will become remains to be seen; yet there is every reason to believe that scientific behavior control has never before played such a large role in our everyday lives and that it never again will play such a small one.

"But why," asks the skeptic, "should scientific methods for controlling human behavior improve?" For these reasons:

1. *Today more scientists are engaged in research relevant to behavior control.* It has recently been estimated that 90 percent of all the scientists who ever lived are alive today, publishing their work in 100,000 scientific journals. A goodly number of these investigators (often the brightest men in their fields) are focusing on behavior control problems. Why? Because such work is particularly fascinating? To aid man in his search for a better destiny? Because research funds are more readily available to investigators conducting such work? Yes, for all these reasons, and one other: Behavior control research

is glamorous research. After all, the person who labors on problems of behavior control delves into matters of the highest public interest. He is likely to become a celebrity of sorts, a man on television or the cover of *Time*. He deals with issues of power and in so doing becomes powerful himself.[7]

2. *Scientific knowledge is cumulative.* Each new generation of scientists starts, not from scratch, but rather from where its elder colleagues left off. One gets a "pyramidal effect" in science—knowledge built upon knowledge—a steady advance into the unknown. And just as surely as yesterday's Model T led to today's Thunderbird, so will today's behavior control technology lead to a more sophisticated, more effective behavior control technology tomorrow.

3. *Behavior control research has an interdisciplinary flavor.* One of the best ways to advance our understanding of a problem or subject is to attack it from several scientific points of view at once. When, for instance, biology, psychology, chemistry, engineering, sociology, and physics join forces in common pursuit of some elusive answer, there is a better chance that an answer will be found. This is because the interdisciplinary approach allows for a cross-fertilization of scientific ideas and suggests ways for combining scientific knowledge in accomplishing a specified objective. The U.S. space program is a good example. To get man and spaceship to a specified objective and back requires a scope of knowledge too broad to be encompassed by one scientific discipline. That is why the National Aeronautics and Space Administration hires scientists from many fields to plan and execute space probes. The interdisciplinary approach to the science of behavior control is just beginning. As it gathers momentum so will progress in the control of human behavior.

4. *Methodological advances have furthered the study of behavior control and facilitated the implementation of behavior control technology in society.* The famous nineteenth century French physiologist, Claude Bernard, is credited with this important insight:

I am convinced, in experimental sciences that are evolving, . . . discovery of a new tool for observation or experiment is much more useful than any number of systematic or philosophic dissertations. Indeed, a new method or a new means of investigation increases our power and makes discoveries and researches possible which would not have been possible without its help.

Never was Bernard's belief more applicable than in the evolving science of behavior control, where numerous examples exist of methodological advances bringing about new insights into the regulation of human conduct.

The course of brain stimulation research provides an exceptionally fine example of how methodological advances lead to marked progress in behavior control. To begin with, even rudimentary work in brain stimulation was not possible before a supporting methodology was developed: specific surgical tools, sophisticated implantation techniques, fine electrodes that could deliver minute quantities of electrical or chemical stimuli to the depths of the brain, histological procedures and recording equipment for measuring behavioral responses to brain stimulation.

As brain stimulation methodology improved, so did brain stimulation. It became a more potent behavior control technique. What at first had been a cumbersome process—an animal or human chained to the stimulating apparatus by wires—evolved into a convenient process whereby an organism could receive stimulation at the push of a button while he was free to roam about at will, unfettered by connecting wires.

Dr. Delgado who, you will recall, used brain stimulation with humans to induce a wide range of motor, intellective, and emotional responses, has been a pioneer in developing brain stimulation equipment and tools. Maybe that is why one of his major addresses was delivered to the Institute of Electrical and Electronics Engineers at their annual convention. Delgado recognizes the importance of methodology in his work. It is methodology, combined with scientific insight, that is turning behavior control from a speculative possibility into a practical reality.

5. *There is social support for the development of behavior control systems.* When the average American depends on science to make him healthy, happy, and wholesome—in short, to make life easier and more enjoyable—he doesn't always realize that he is supporting research in behavior control. Yet today there is a growing expectation on the part of government and governed alike that scientists have the right and obligation to control human behavior for the good of both citizen and society. The intensity of this expectation is understandable when one realizes that the American's psychological strength, battered in the tumultuous crosscurrents of our changing world, needs outside rejuvenation to propel him through life successfully.

One can observe many socially sanctioned forms of behavior control already functioning in contemporary America: in psychopharmacology, where millions of dollars are spent to tranquilize and energize our populace; in therapy, where thousands of psychologists and psychiatrists try to buoy up the nation's mental health; in computer technology, where hundreds of high-speed, electronic information-processing machines are used to regulate and guide our thoughts.

Americans look to science for direction and aid in living, and as long as they do Professor London will be correct in claiming that contemporary behavior control techniques have been implemented in our society not "by the will of tyrants but by the invitation of all of us, for we have been schooled to readiness for all these things and will demand their benign use regardless of their potential risk" (London, 1969).

## The "Final Revolution": 1776 or 1984?

In 1961, the University of California held a symposium on "Control of the Mind." Dean Saunders of the San Francisco Medical School made headlines when he declared: "It is now possible to act directly on the individual to modify his behavior instead of his environment. This, then, constitutes a part of what Aldous Huxley has called 'The Final Revolution.' "

In the preceding pages of this chapter we have presented a sampling of the advances in behavior control that lead men like Saunders to make such remarks. On one point many scholars are in agreement: an effective system of behavior control will be realized. The only dispute concerns when. If we accept the inevitability of behavior control, then the important question to ask is not whether human actions can be regulated, but what will happen when they are. Even if one is not certain that behavior control will become a reality, it still seems reasonable to play it safe and speculate on what might happen if it does.

How will a sound behavior control technology influence our society and ourselves? In many cases scientists are reluctant to talk in broad social terms, let alone answer the loaded question we have just posed. But such a posture is no longer tenable. The behavioral sciences have advanced to a point where guidelines are necessary and speculation about the social consequences of behavior control required.

It is tragic that, at a time when the understanding of science is of utmost importance, the country—particularly the young people—is being swept up in an antiscience trend. Part of this ground swell of rejection is rooted in a fear of scientific behavior control—a dread of Huxley's "Final Revolution." But, as we asked earlier, is such a revolution necessarily bad? The American revolution brought freedom to Americans; could not Huxley's revolution do the same? Might not man, in learning to control his own behavior, gain the wisdom necessary to construct the peaceful, productive world he so desperately needs?

We will examine these critical questions in the chapters that follow. To do so we will touch on many timeworn controversies, especially the conflict between freedom and determinism. It is the fashion today to begin a discussion of free will by apologizing for bringing up an ancient problem. This curious attitude is made more striking by the fact that the literature on this "ancient problem" has expanded geometrically during the past decade! We make no apology for discussing free will. The concept of freedom is central to Western civilization. If scientific behavior control threatens to destroy traditional concepts of free choice and free will, then scientists have a responsibility to discuss the implications of their work. In the words of Shakespeare:

> The weight of this sad time we must obey,
> Speak what we feel, not what we ought to say.

# LIVING WITH THE
# 2 FAUSTIAN POWER

*Social science today is as much feared as a*
*hidden persuader or manipulator of man*
*as a generation ago it was admired as a*
*liberator.*

David Riesman

The fear of powerful new knowledge is a human reflex of long standing. It is reflected in the myths of Prometheus, Icarius, Dr. Faustus, and of the tree of knowledge in the Garden of Eden. It is not surprising, then, that famed political scientist Herman Kahn should refer to the technology of behavior control as a "Faustian power." Nor is it surprising that such power should be regarded as evil. "Those who have explicitly avowed an interest in control have been roughly treated by history," notes Skinner. "Machiavelli is the great prototype. As Macaulay said of him, 'Out of his surname they coined an epithet for a knave and out of his Christian name a synonym for the devil'" (Rogers & Skinner, 1956).

In contemporary America the fear of new knowledge is reinforced by the myth of the omnipotent scientist—the person endowed with awesome powers created in superlaboratories. That such people do not exist hardly seems to matter.

37

John Q. Public persists in speculating that men armed with scientific know-how might be able to make anyone do anything.

The citizen can hardly be blamed for his unrest. His fear of scientific behavior control has been nurtured on a diet of exaggerations and half-truths from overzealous reporters, inflammatory pseudoscience writers, imaginative novelists, flamboyant scientists, and government alarmists. Why shouldn't he be uneasy? He hears vague references to brainwashing, truth serums, and hypnosis.[8] He reads novels like 1984 and *Brave New World,* which describe awesome behavior control procedures such as socialization by aversive conditioning, chemical "stunting" of normal brain growth, mass use of lobotomy operations, and the attachment of human brains to computers by micro-surgery. If he prefers nonfiction, *The Hidden Persuaders, Battle for the Mind, The Rape of the Mind,* and *The Brain Watchers* treat him to some unsettling prophecies (Karlins & Abelson, 1970). The "danger" of behavior control is constantly exploited on television in such science-fiction operas as *Outer Limits, The Invaders, Man from UNCLE,* and *Mission Impossible.* And Mary Shelley's *Frankenstein,* which is revived every few years by Hollywood, is a constant reminder to movie audiences of the "evil" inherent in behavioral engineering.

Now it is certainly true that the technology of behavior control should not be taken lightly. We will argue that it has profound implications for society. But some of the current fears concerning the scientific control of behavior are fears with little or no factual basis. In order to face the real problems of the Faustian power, we must dispel three *unwarranted* assumptions many Americans hold about behavior control.

1. *Man would be free in the absence of scientific behavior control.* In a famous speech before the American Psychological Association, the late Dr. Robert Oppenheimer (1956) warned that "the psychologist can hardly do anything without realizing that for him the acquisition of knowledge opens up

the most terrifying prospects of controlling what people do and how they think and how they behave and how they feel." Implicit in Oppenheimer's statement is the idea that in the absence of behavioral science man is somehow "free." What follows from this is the fear that most forms of scientific behavior control are intrinsically evil because they deprive man of freedom.

We cannot deal rationally with the behavioral sciences until we realize that control per se is not even an issue. From the scientist's viewpoint, all human actions follow laws and patterns, just as physical events do, and are, in that sense, controlled. Behavior control techniques do not impose a "scientific straitjacket" on human behavior; they merely replace the so-called normal influences of nature and society, which may include arbitrary parents, incompetent teachers, unrealistic TV programs, and chemically polluted food. As Nobel Laureate Joshua Lederberg has argued, abolishing the study and manipulation of human behavior would not alter the fact that man responds in consistent ways to his environment. The real question is not "Should man be controlled?" but "How should he be controlled?" By the erratic forces of nature, or by man himself?

The world is, in a sense, one large "Skinner Box," or behavior control laboratory. The contents of a man's environment—his parents and friends, his house and clothing, his food and medicines, his tools and appliances—are the mechanisms by which his behavior is modified and directed. Skinner has frequently pointed out how people living together in groups consciously and unconsciously control each other's actions. When an individual behaves in a fashion approved by the group, he receives admiration, approval, affection, and many other reinforcements that increase the likelihood that he will continue to behave in the same fashion. Similarly, when he behaves in a disapproved fashion, rewards are withdrawn or punishment is applied. Dissenters and nonconformists are not "free" of control; many have simply internalized a divergent program of attitudes and responses as a consequence of peculiar childhood and adolescent conditioning experiences. The relationship between early experience and student radicalism, for example, is carefully documented by Yale psychologist Kenneth Keniston in his highly acclaimed study of *The Young Radicals.*

The knowledge that all behavior follows consistent scientific laws is hard to accept. As Dostoevsky put it:

> Out of sheer ingratitude man will play you a dirty trick, just to prove that men are still men and not the keys of a piano. . . . And even if you could prove that man is only a piano key, he would still do something out of sheer perversity—he would create destruction and chaos—just to gain his point. . . . And if all of this could in turn be analyzed and prevented by prediction that it would occur, then man would go absolutely mad to prove his point (Dostoevsky, as quoted in Skinner, 1955–1956).

Psychologist Abraham Maslow (1966) has also commented on man's resentment of the notion that he is predictable. In one book, he cites the case of "a ten-year-old girl, known for always being a good citizen, law-abiding and dutiful [who] unexpectedly disrupted classroom discipline by passing out French fried potatoes instead of notebooks because, as she later said, everyone just took her good behavior for granted." As the distinguished scholar Ludwig Immergluck (1964) has pointed out, the notion that man is "a free agent propelled by self-initiated inner forces that defy, by their very nature, prediction or scientifically ordered description" seems to be a necessary illusion. But it is an illusion! Behavioral science does not create special biological and psychological laws in order to control man; it deals with patterns that already exist in nature.

2. *The scientific control of behavior is evil.* Once we realize that all behavior is controlled, it follows that the tech-

nology of behavior control is not good or bad, but neutral. To say that behavior control is evil is like condemning atomic physics. An atomic reaction can light a city or burn it. The problem is not the technology, but how man chooses to use it. There is a certain irony in the science of behavior control: as it develops the power to free men's minds from excessive worry (such as through therapy), it also gains the means to enslave their thoughts. Like the atom, the science of behavior control is neutral. Man will determine whether research findings will be used to liberate or to subjugate the human spirit, to serve or to destroy, to cure or to infect.

Since the popular arts have given so much attention to deleterious applications of behavioral science, we wish to stress its positive potential. Doctors have practiced behavioral control on a limited scale for centuries, using medicines to remedy diseases and bodily malfunctions. It is doubtful that a person cured of a once-fatal disease such as polio would complain that his freedom to die had been violated! Biomedical researchers are now working on ways to cure heart disease, cancer, and genetically induced defects, such as dwarfism, hemophilia, and assorted allergies. Psychologists are actively seeking ways to improve man's mental health, memory, and creative potential—all necessary attributes if man wishes to survive in his demanding, rapidly changing world.

Experiments at the University of Chicago and the Langley Neurosychiatric Institute are aimed directly at employing behavioral science to free man from external and internal forces. Student subjects are trained to exercise conscious control over the production of alpha waves—waves measured by the EEG (electroencephalogram) that are associated with states of tranquility. Psychologist Joseph Kamiya suggests that if different subjective states—anxiety, misery, euphoria, and tranquility—can be mapped out and linked with specific brain states as measured by the EEG, people could be trained to control their moods at will. People in full control of their internal conscious states would be well prepared to resist coercion. Even Carl Rogers, who at times has been cynical about the benefits of a human control technology, concedes that "the behavioral sciences could move toward the release of potentialities and capacities. I think that there is enough work already done to indicate that one can set up conditions which release behavior that is more variable, more spontaneous, more creative, and hence in its specifics, more unpredictable" (Rogers, 1961).

Those who equate behavior control with evil frequently refer to Aldous Huxley's *Brave New World* to substantiate their arguments. On the issue of control, Huxley is frequently misinterpreted. It is instructive to compare *Brave New World* with *Island,* one of Huxley's later novels. Both describe programmed societies, but with different results. In *Brave New World,* people use technology to distract and enslave themselves. In *Island* the same technology is employed to advance human awareness and to broaden the scope of human action.

We do not overlook the possibility that behavior control is dangerous in an accidental sense. If we can draw an analogy to ecology, we must recognize that the human animal is a delicate eco-system and that any attempt to change his behavior in a systematic way should be carefully controlled for possible side effects. But the caution necessary in experiments with humans does not lead to the conclusion that control per se is bad. If it did, medicine would still be in the hands of tribal witch doctors.

3. *Only scientists or politicians can use behavior control technology to regulate human conduct.* There is always the danger, of course, that unscrupulous men in science or government might try to employ behavior control technology on a mass scale to impose their will on the American public. Today such a possibility is remote simply because regulatory procedures are not yet powerful enough to sway a nation full of unwilling minds without the active involvement of millions of scientific or political conspirators.

*At this point in the developing science of behavior con-*

*trol, the real potential for irresponsible use of the Faustian power resides not with a tyrannical government or elite corps of scientists, but rather with individuals who employ behavior control technology on a personal or interpersonal basis.* (This is the reason psychologists are licensed.) It is at this "local" level that regulatory procedures difficult to implement on a mass scale become effective.

An example of interpersonal abuse is the case of two students who decided to change an athlete roommate, by conditioning, into an art lover. They hung various pictures on the walls and, knowing their friend liked attention, deprived him of it. They ignored him completely, unless he happened to be noticing a picture. Within a week the roommate was talking about the pictures all the time. The conversion was complete when he got up one morning and said, "Hey, fellows, how about going to the museum?" (Wald, 1965).

Many doctors, noting the widespread use of tranquilizers and antidepressants, have warned that people may unknowingly lock themselves into self-imposed drug prisons. In a frightening article in the *Atlantic* (1966), journalist Bruce Jackson describes the refreshments at a middle-class pill party:

> Next to the candy dish filled with Dexedrine, Dexamyl, Eskatrol, Desbutal, and a few other products I haven't yet learned to identify, near the five-pound box of Dexedrine tablets someone had brought, were two bottles. One was filled with Dexedrine Elixir, the other with Dexamyl Elixer.

Those who attend such parties are "well educated (largely college graduates), are older (25 to 40), and middle class (with a range of occupations: writers, artists, lawyers, TV executives, journalists, political aides, housewives)." The mere existence of drugs does not rob an individual of his autonomy, but it does give him the option of surrendering it. If, then, he evolves into a contented cow, it will not be because he is manipulated by a clique of omnipotent rulers. It will be because he has decided that there is nothing more worthwhile than "grazine."

## No Escape from Freedom

The problem posed by behavior control is not external tyranny. On the contrary, the real problem is the threat of freedom. If we take the deterministic stance and agree with neurophysiologist Ralph W. Gerard that "there can be no twisted thought without a twisted molecule," and if we recognize that a perfected behavior control technology is within our grasp, then for the first time in history we are truly responsible for our destiny. Or as Julian Huxley put it, man is now, in effect, "managing director of the business of evolution" with no possibility of losing the job. Whether he chooses to approach the problem or to let things drift, he makes a choice. Ironically, the deterministic science of man has burdened him with the hardest problem of all: freedom. In short, there are no more excuses for human misery. If man has the knowledge to create Julian Huxley's "fulfillment society," he can only blame himself if he produces anything less.

If the notion that determinism is liberating seems a paradox, we must recognize the extent to which tyrants have abused the concept of freedom in order to exact rigid social compliance from others. If man has free will, the tyrant argues, then he is responsible—that is, punishable—for not complying with the dictates of the social elite. Indeed, "freedom" is often a tool of repressive societies, both religious and secular. The early Christian leaders, for example, had to postulate human free will within the context of Divine determinism in order to maintain control over the laity. Saint Augustine records his difficulty in disciplining a group of libertine monks whose claim to innocence was that their actions were "fated by an omnipotent God." The Russians have recently faced the same problem. Immediately after the Russian revolution, the Soviets rejected introspectionist psychologies because they smacked of free will, which contradicted Marxist determinism. By the forties, however, the Soviets found it necessary to incorporate concepts of freedom into their psychology in order to justify increasing authoritarian suppression. Freedom was defined as "the recognition of necessity" by consciousness. This doctrine, in addition to resolving Marxism with voluntarism, served political purposes:

> By postulating that conscious man is free from the determination of the immediate situation, it makes him responsible for his immediate behavior. By stating that consciousness is the understanding of relationships and that "freedom is the recognition of necessity," it offers a rationale for the subjugation of the individual to the demands of society (Bauer, 1952).

History is rife with examples of tyrannical forces relying on the assumption of free will. As Skinner has observed, "The state is frequently defined in terms of power to punish, and jurisprudence leans heavily upon the associated notion of personal responsibility" (Skinner, 1955–1956).

In 1941, Erich Fromm wrote an influential book entitled *Escape from Freedom*. Its theme is familiar to any student of social science: "Modern man, freed from the bonds of traditional societies, has security, but is restrained by his desire to escape from freedom. Freedom, though it has brought him independence and rationality, has made him isolated and, thereby, anxious and powerless" (Fromm, 1941). The technology of behavior control has made escape impossible. Whatever man does, even if he burns all the behavioral science textbooks, he is choosing his ultimate destiny. Man fears the behavioral sciences, not only because they threaten to enslave him, but because—even more frightening—they threaten to free him. As Ernest Becker (1968) writes in the *Structure of Evil*, "The question that our civilization is now asked to face is whether we are ready to make man the master of his social games, rather than their unwitting servant."

# TWO VISIONS

*Give me Librium or give me meth.*
  Graffiti
  New York, 1971

*This is the dawning of the Age of Aquarius.*
  "Aquarius"

The Faustian power gives man the ability to control his destiny, but it doesn't tell him what he should aim for. The contemporary American has two visions of how his society should be organized. Behavior control technology can be used to *facilitate* and *accelerate* the development of either one. This is the importance of the Faustian power: it can, and will, play a large role in the evolution of American political traditions.

## Two Visions of Democracy

The next decade will witness a struggle for supremacy between two forms of social organization in the United States and the rest of the industrialized world. These forms have been identified under various rubrics by an impressive array of social scientists, including Erich Fromm, John Kenneth Galbraith, David Reisman, Kenneth Keniston, Theodore Roszak, Jacques Ellul, and William H. White. For the sake of simplicity, we will designate them *organizational democracy* and *participatory democracy*.

Organizational democracy is the logical outgrowth of the present social and industrial order. The term describes a society where economic and political organization is progressively concentrated and centralized, where efficiency and economy are emphasized above quality, and where a de facto scientific and technological caste system operates. The goal of an organizational democracy is the smooth functioning of the prevailing socioeconomic order, and consequently the role of the individual is defined as "fitting in" or "finding his proper place."

Participatory democracy is a reaction to the prevailing organizational trend that seeks to realize the neo-Jeffersonian ideal of a genuinely free society composed of flexible, responsible units. The goal of a participatory democracy is individual fulfillment, and consequently it designs social organizations to meet the diverse needs and aspirations of individuals operating within them.

## The Technological Machine

Organizational democracy is the technological extension of our bureaucratic society. Like sociologist Robert Merton's (1949) definition of a bureaucracy, organizational democracy is characterized by a clear-cut division of activities within institutions on the basis of technical competence, by the existence of complex rules governing behavior, and by "the constant use of *categorization* whereby individual problems and cases are classified on the basis of designated criteria and are treated ac-

cordingly." But organizational democracy goes beyond the
basic bureaucratic model; it seeks to organize the whole of society so that all of its parts (including people) perform as one
smooth-running, self-maintaining machine. In the words of
Theodore Roszak, organizational democracy (he calls it *tech-
nocracy*) is

> . . . the ideal men usually have in mind when they speak of
> modernizing, up-dating, rationalizing, planning. Drawing up-
> on such unquestionable imperatives as the demand for effi-
> ciency, for social security, for large-scale coordination of men
> and resources, for ever higher levels of affluence and ever more
> impressive manifestations of collective human power, [the
> technocracy] works to knit together the anachronistic gaps
> and fissures of the industrial society. . . . Politics, education,
> leisure, entertainment, culture as a whole, unconscious drives,
> and even . . . protest against the technocracy itself: all these
> become the subjects of purely technical scrutiny and of purely
> technical manipulation. The effort is to create a new social
> organism whose health depends upon its capacity to keep the
> technological heart beating rapidly (Roszak, 1969).

People are not only regarded as parts of the social machine,
but the most flexible and consequently the most malleable
and interchangeable parts. When a technical innovation, such
as the computer, promises to increase efficiency, schools are
rapidly established to retain, or redesign, the people or the
parts, to accommodate the demands of the innovation.

Descriptions of the evolving organizational democracy
vary, depending on the politics and academic perspective of
the writer. Galbraith, for example, will concentrate on economic organization, while Marcuse will stress the structure of
social thought. However, the following characteristics can be
identified:

First, *social influence flows from the top downward.* In
the economic sphere, for example, a decision as to what will

be produced does not come from the consumer. "Rather it comes from the great producing organization which reaches forward to control the market that it is presumed to serve and, beyond, to bend the consumer to its needs" (Galbraith, 1967). Galbraith cites as an example the production of the Ford Mustang, which required over three years to design at a tooling cost of over 50 million dollars. Because of the time required to complete the task, the high amount of capital committed, and the complexity of organized talent brought to bear on the production of the Mustang, the public could not be trusted to make a rational choice about the car. In order to insure that the Mustang—and, thereby, the social machine— would be successful, the people had to be conditioned by advertising to want the car.

Second, *the range of human experience is restricted.*[9] As society grows more centralized and technical, social survival requires that the individual become more and more specialized in his day-to-day activities. It is not enough to be a lawyer, or even a *securities* lawyer: a person must become a *municipal bond securities* lawyer. Similarly, a "successful" medical man is not a doctor, or even a dermatologist, or even an allergist; he is an allergist who specializes in pollen (or animal dander, dust, and so on).

Much is said these days, especially at universities, about the interdisciplinarian—the man who, according to popular myth, transcends his speciality by bridging two or more fields. Such a description gives us the illusion that the interdisciplinarian is a person with broad outlook and abilities. In reality, the hyphenate (for example, the lawyer-engineer) has narrowed his vision to include *only* those small areas where his chosen fields intersect. The lawyer-engineer is not a general counsel and a versatile engineer combined in one; he is a specialist in engineering law. People who are required to maintain a broad outlook, such as high-level corporation executives, university presidents, and other administrators, actually possess little power. They are most often called upon to manage the outcomes of events over which they have exercised little control. As industrial psychologist Warren Bennis (1970) explains, "Paradoxically, the higher one goes the more tethered and bound he feels by expectations and commitments." In sum, organizational democracy demonstrates a unique caste system in which the individual gains status and freedom by narrowing the range and scope of his activities.

Specialization leads to a third characteristic of organizational democracy: *conformity and the suppression of individual impulses.* The very process of specialization requires intensive disipline and submission to professional rules and codes. But this is just the beginning. A lawyer, doctor, engineer, electrician, or programmer may experience freedom within the confines of his speciality, but the very fact of his expertise locks him into cooperation with other experts. As William White (1961) has noted, large and complex organizations demand that "the way in which each specialist presents his information and the kinds of questions he must answer depend on his fitting the information in with that of other specialists." Furthermore, as organizations themselves become increasingly specialized, the individual is compelled to conform to an even narrower range of alternatives. "When we talk of pressures for uniformity," writes Murray Hausknecht (1957), "we are saying in effect that it is increasingly difficult for individuals to bring their own distinctive styles to their social roles. We are saying that it is becoming harder to seize upon the ambiguities which pervade all spheres of action and use them to explore other alternatives, because the disciplines are becoming so narrow as to eliminate these ambiguities."

This trend toward conformity receives legitimacy from the ethic that social progress supersedes all. Those who suffer the "illness" of deviating from social norms are "healed" by psychiatrists and psychologists who, despite the strident protests of a professional minority, equate psychic normalcy with conformity. This is, of course, a powerful influence. Who can fight back at science?

The fourth characteristic of organizational democracy is the voluntary *surrender of individual autonomy* for professional management. Since everyone is encouraged to be an expert in some area, everyone is, in one sense, a manager. But each person's specialty is so narrow that he is more the managed than he is the manager. In short, an organizational democracy is a society where everyone is at once a part-time master and a full-time slave. There are no bosses; indeed, as we have seen, the broad administrator has less autonomy than the highly specialized technician. The system is interdependent and self-perpetuating. It is democratic in the sense that people are programmed to respond to what the system affords. People choose what they want, but their wants are determined by the boundaries of the social machine.

This brings us to the final and most pervasive characteristic of organizational democracy: *technology, not human happiness, is the ultimate source of values.* Not that happiness is ignored. But it is viewed from the perspective of social progress. Happiness is not an end in itself, but simply the means to the efficient functioning of the social machine. For example, in *Up the Organization,* a best-selling guide to corporate gamesmanship, former Avis chief Robert Townsend recommends that executives be allowed to keep their own hours. Not because it makes them happier—which it does—but because such ostensible permissiveness makes them more efficient producers. Happiness for the sake of joy, on the other hand, is tantamount to sin, especially when it interferes with progress. Even the student radicals are infected with the notion that time deducted from "business as usual" must be used productively, that is, in the interest of some social project or cause such as ecology. We have yet to hear a political group agitate for a day of free time just for the fun of having one more day to ourselves.

## The Evolution of Psytocracy

> *In the end they will lay their freedom at*
> *our feet and say to us, "make us your slaves,*
> *but feed us."*
>
> Dostoevsky
> *The Grand Inquisitor*

As our organizational democracy becomes increasingly centralized owing to large-scale planning and as cybernation becomes a major instrument of control, maximum technical efficiency increasingly overshadows optimal human development as the ultimate social goal. People judge their own "progress" in terms of how they can best relate to social goals and expectations. One consequence of this is that individuals become passive; they surrender their seemingly insignificant autonomy to the authority of Society, allowing themselves to be molded by it for fear of being overwhelmed instead. A clear manifestation of this trend is the growing popularity of what might best be called the How to Live literature, books and magazine articles that tell people how to relate better to each other. How to Make Your Husband Happy. How to Understand Your Tripped-out Teen-ager. How to Respond When Your Spouse Wants a Divorce. And so on. The American is becoming so attuned to external authority that he is anesthetizing his senses. He is so cut off from his emotional core that he must depend on popular psychology to negotiate his most intimate personal experiences.

Youthful dissenters also display a curious dependency on external authority and sanction. Psychologists and psychiatrists point out that many radicals suffer from deep feelings of inadequacy and worthlessness. On one level they reject social approval, but on another they have an intense need to prove their worth by doing good in the eyes of their peers. Keniston (1968) makes the interesting observation that many reform-minded young adults were once successful, status-conscious adolescents. Without deprecating the useful and long overdue reform efforts of many students and graduates, we might hypothesize that these dissenters have not abandoned what Riesman called "other-directed" behavior, but have simply switched reference groups, from parents to peers.

Given enough time, organizational democracy will evolve into what we referred to in the first chapter as a *psytocracy*, a society where all things, including people "things," are subject to careful and precise technical manipulation. In order to secure the success of long-range social planning, individual variability is restricted to predictable and manageable channels. A psytocracy is a form of tyranny, but not in the classical sense of the word. The slaves and the masters are indistinguishable. Each person is so conditioned to social norms and values that he eagerly performs whatever the social machine demands. The tyranny is not the external force of coercion but the internal force of a well-developed social superego. In a psytocracy there is no dissent because everyone defines freedom in the same terms, for example, the freedom to do gleefully what is expected of him.

In this sense, a psytocracy would be no different in the United States, the Soviet Union, or Communist China. People would spout different catch phrases, but their behavior would be the same—to service the prevailing technological order.


## The Humanistic Revolt

Needless to say, organizational democracy and the spectre of psytocracy have not been highly praised by academic and other intellectuals. Organizational democracy requires that the individual be molded to fit the overall social goals; and intellectuals, who as critics are professional outsiders, are particularly sensitive to pressures for conformity.

But intellectuals are not alone in their dissent. The accelerating trends of centralization, cybernation, and regimentation have produced dissatisfaction among less articulate—though often more vocal—members of society. We are all familiar with the alienation that exists among young, especially college students and dropouts. This is not a new development; it dates back to the "beat" phenomenon of the early fifties, as chronicled by Paul Goodman in *Growing Up Absurd*.

More recent, and more significant, dissent has come from industrial psychologists and from members of the organizational structure itself. Warren Bennis, of the State University of New York at Buffalo, and Chris Argyris, of Yale, two of the country's leading psychologists, maintain that the conflict between the needs of organizational democracy and an individual businessman's needs for diversity and control over his destiny is creating a growing dissatisfaction among corporate executives. In a pyramidal organizational structure the executive feels that few of his abilities will be used and, consequently, that his needs for success and self-esteem will not be met. Paul Kurtz identifies the emergence of *nonconforming ambivalents:*

> Their behavior is ambivalent, for they cannot accommodate to the system or play by the role required of them. Unable to accept the status system or the [organization's] goals, such individuals rebel against it and may be eventually forced to leave. Nonconformists may be anomic or highly idealistic in motivation. The idealist within the [organization] constantly harbors guilt feelings and suffers the disparity between the ideal and the actual. Unable to fit into the organization, he may flee to the academy, the church, or to the arts. Though here he may soon discover, much to his consternation, that big [organization] is again presently attempting to organize his talents, and that compromise with some organization is the fact of his existence. If he is to write, he needs a publisher. If he is to preach, a pulpit; if he is to teach, a school. Alas, the individual can scarcely survive outside of an organization

without becoming entirely helpless and ineffectual; yet, within it he is often smothered (Kurtz, 1969).

The result of dissatisfaction among intellectuals, the young, and a growing number of "nonconformist ambivalents" is a reaction to organizational democracy. It is a call for *participatory democracy*—that is, for a social system that seeks to *cultivate* and *serve* the needs of people, rather than to design people to serve the system.

It is important here to differentiate participatory democracy from "the hippie dream." The two are often confused, even by those who advocate participatory democracy. As Yablonsky points out, the hippie dream is tantamount to regression. It longs

> . . . to return to the tribal position of the American Indian or the more satisfying life of a more closely knit extended family—a situation where adults and children can live more intimately and humanely in a cohesive face-to-face primary group. The goal, therefore, is a more cohesive, emotionally closer, fundamental human unit living in a more natural state (Yablonsky, 1968).

As Keniston observes, hippies and their sympathizers commit the fallacy of romantic regression:

> One of the most common reactions against technological society is to deplore it by invoking images of a romanticized past as a guidepost for regressive social change. . . . This ideology starts from the valid observation that our postindustrial society has lost intact community, socially given identity, stable and accepted morality, certainty, and a clear collective sense of direction. From this valid observation, the regressive position attempts to re-establish a simple "organic" community, long for Jeffersonian agrarianism, seeks a "new conservatism" which will "preserve" the values of the nineteenth century, turns to Fascism with its appeal to blood feeling and "the corporate state," or is tempted by the syndicalist vision of

re-attaining "genuine" self-governing communities of workers (Keniston, 1960).

What hippies forget is that "harsher realities lie behind these romanticized images: endemic disease, grinding poverty, high infant mortality, lawlessness, and often the most elementary requirements for subsistence." Although organizational democracy suppresses individual variation, it does provide basic services. We must also remember that bureaucracy, with all its faults, arose with good reason. It provided security. It was a reaction to the arbitrary and inhuman practices that passed for management science in the early days of the industrial revolution.

Ferdinand Toennis (1855–1936), one of history's most influential social scientists, differentiated between primary emotional relationships of traditional society (*Gemeinschaft*) and the impersonal, contracted relationships of modern society (*Gesellschaft*). Participatory democracy seeks *neo-gemeinschaft,* but not through regression. Rather, it seeks to "humanize" technology, as described by Erich Fromm in 1968:

> While in alienated bureaucracy all power flows from above downward, in humanistic management there is a two-way street; the "subjects" of the decision made above respond accordingly to their own will and concerns; their response not only reaches the top decision makers but forces them to respond in turn. The "subjects" of decision making have a right to challenge the decision makers. Such a challenge would first of all require a rule that if a sufficient number of "subjects" demanded that the corresponding bureaucracy (on whatever level) answer questions, explain its procedures, the decision makers would respond to the demand.

Humanistic technology, according to Fromm, is characterized by "active participation of the citizen in the decision-making process, and by finding ways and methods by which government planning is controlled by those for whom the planning is done."

Participatory democracy does not deny leadership; it merely seeks to make leadership respond to the needs of the people it serves. Organizations exist for the sake of human beings; human beings do not exist for the sake of organizations. The goal of educational development is revised from fitting the man to the machine to finding the opportunity in the economy that brings out the man, and if the opportunity does not exist, to make it This involves encouraging individual enterprises and perhaps even subsidizing nonconformity. The impersonalization of the organizational democracy is remedied by giving workers more voice in production and the kind of training to make that voice wise.

Participatory democracy is more than a reaction to organizational democracy: they are antithetical institutions. Participatory democracy is a heresy in a society that suppresses spontaneity for the sake of impersonal service to large and centralized organizations, a society that is essentialist rather than existentialist. For this reason, participatory democracy has been practiced so far only on a limited scale and primarily in university communities. The Free Schools at Berkeley, Stanford, and Harvard are one manifestation. Community Control programs, many of which are funded by the Office of Economic Opportunity, are another. A nonacademic experiment in participatory democracy is Twin Oaks, an experimental community in central Virginia. It was founded by people who admire the community concepts set forth in *Walden Two*. Work is distributed equitably among all members. A labor credit system, patterned after the one in *Walden Two*, attempts to give each participant as much choice of jobs as possible and to adjust work loads in accord with the desirability of the job. Even in the business community there are some stirrings of participatory democracy. Businessmen, especially in the communications and consulting industries, have begun to realize that "the need for autonomy and independence may be a more deep-seated human motive than is recognized by those who characterize our society in terms of crowd-like conformity and the decline of individualism" (Blauner, 1960). This awareness is reflected in loose and flexible organizational structures.

## Democracy and Behavior Control

It was our intention in this chapter to outline briefly [10] two visions of postindustrial American society: psytocracy, in which individuals are molded to fit the prevailing social order, and participatory democracy, in which the institutions serve the individual by cultivating, as well as responding to, his unique potentialities. We do not imply an absolute dichotomy between these two forms of social organization. All societies must exact some conformity in order to maintain social order; similarly, even the most rigid societies must promote some degree of variability in order to maintain the different parts of the complex social machine. The difference between organizational democracy and participatory democracy is one of emphasis, but that emphasis is critically important: the supremacy of social stability versus the supremacy of individual expression. In reflecting on this distinction, specific points should be kept in mind.

First, the traditional conception of a democracy as a government that guarantees free expression of ideas and behavior is meaningless for the purposes of comparing organizational and participatory democracies. As much as we might deplore *Brave New World,* we should remember that its citizens were completely free to do and say whatever they wished. They were not overtly forced to conform; they had been conditioned *to want to conform.* If democracy is to have any meaning, it must not be defined simply in terms of wants, which are malleable, but in terms of human potential. That is, a psytoc-racy is less democratic than a participatory democracy in the sense that it restricts the possible range of behaviors within each person. This revised notion of democracy was first used by Erich Fromm in *Escape from Freedom* and more recently by Herbert Marcuse in *One-Dimensional Man*. It is a difficult concept for those who experienced traditional totalitarianism before World War II to understand and is, undoubtedly, a conceptual wedge in the so-called generation gap.

Second, participatory democracy does not nullify the laws of behavioral science. A person living in a participatory democracy is just as much a product of biological and psycho-logical forces as the person living in an organizational democ-racy; the difference is in how the laws of behavior are applied. In an organizational democracy, the individual is rewarded for conformity and constriction of behavior; in a participatory de-mocracy, he is rewarded for expressing as much independence and behavioral flexibility as his genetic potential will allow. In both cases, *behavior is controlled*.

Finally, the technology of behavior control will not arbi-trarily determine which vision of the future will finally mater-ialize. The forces that perpetuate organizational democracy are the desires for security, status, and social approval; they are not the product of genetic engineering, of drug and chemi-cal control of the brain, or of a planned program of condition-ing. Similarly, the pressures for participatory democracy are the desires for autonomy, for spontaneous expression, and for varied experience. The techniques of behavior control can be used to advance either organizational or participatory democ-racy. They will play a significant, but *supportive,* role in de-termining social destiny; that is, they will *facilitate and accel-erate* either trend. Once people have decided in which direction they will move, they will then voluntarily employ behavioral science in the service of that decision. Again the analogy to physics is useful. Atomic physics does not cause nuclear war or create low-cost atomic power plants. Physics is a tool used by men who have already decided whether to build a civilization or to destroy it.

In which direction will society move? Toward participatory democracy with its emphasis on human individuality and initiative, or toward psytocracy with its emphasis on human conformity and passivity? Before we can answer that question we must first examine the psychological condition of the twentieth century American.

# REFLECTIONS ON THE
# 4 AMERICAN CHARACTER
# WHILE STANDING IN A
# NEW YORK
# SUBWAY STATION

*. . . and the words of the prophets are*
*written on the subway walls.*

Simon and Garfunkel
"The Sound of Silence"

## What Is the Condition of the Twentieth Century American?

In 1960 Paul Blackburn published *Meditation on the BMT*. There is more to the poem's title than first meets the eye—as we shall soon see. The BMT is a subway line in New York City which is best characterized as a purgatory for commuters. It features dank, filthy stations; uncertain schedules; battered, drafty cars; and body-rattling rides unmatched even by the Long Island Railroad. It also features some pretty unhappy passengers—as George Tooker deftly illustrates in his painting *The Subway* (Plate 1).

The subway rider is important to Blackburn and Tooker because he starkly symbolizes the condition of the twentieth century American. In his hapless plight he becomes an eloquent representative of the malaise that is pervasive in our society. The subway rider is, in this sense, Everyman, and knowing this, one should not be surprised to learn that many people experience a feeling of *déjà vu* ("Haven't I seen those facial expressions before?") when first viewing *The Subway*. Tooker has depicted far more than the empty, frightened faces of subway riders in his work; he has captured on canvas the psychological and emotional state of modern man—what it *is* and how it *feels* to be a modern man—and in so doing has allowed us to respond intellectually and emotionally to the experience he portrays.

How might we label the condition of twentieth century life that Tooker graphically conveys? What term best defines the state of being that is reflected in the hollow, anxious faces of the subway riders? Blackburn's poem suggests an answer. When we realize that "BMT" can also be read as "Be Empty," then we understand that "Meditation on the BMT" is really a "Meditation on Being Empty." And when we speak of being empty—in subways or other ways—we are referring to a human experience found in *alienated* individuals.

## The Alienated American: From the Horatio Alger Myth to the Willie Loman Reality

"If you want to feel alienated," one insurance executive suggested, "take a course in recent American history." Certainly one can appreciate such a viewpoint—particularly when watching the evening news is deemed an act of courage. This has not been an easy century for Americans. Unprecedented change. A depression. Inflation. The generation gap. Riots. Pollution. A war to end all wars. A second war to end all wars. The threat of a third war to end all wars (and everything else, for that matter). "Skirmishes" in Korea, Vietnam, and Cambodia. And superimposed on all these hardships, like an oppressive weight on the human spirit, is the growing sense of alienation and despair that seems to be replacing self-confidence and optimism as the American way of life. Not even the moon-walkers or the Mets seem able to shore up the American spirit and breath life into the American dream.

Today it seems that almost all Americans are alienated from someone or something: blacks from whites; youth from "The Establishment"; workers from jobs; husbands from wives; churchgoers from God; citizens from government; and even the individual from himself! Often man finds himself cut off from his fellow man—in desperate need of human companionship but unable to "make contact." This is the condition eloquently described by Edward Field in his poem *Unwanted*.

The poster with my picture on it
Is hanging on the bulletin board in the Post Office.

I stand by it hoping to be recognized
Posing first full face and then profile

But everybody passes by and I have to admit
The photograph was taken some years ago.

I was unwanted then and I'm unwanted now
Ah guess ah'll go up echo mountain and crah.

I wish someone would find my fingerprints somewhere
Maybe on a corpse and say, You're it.

Description: Male, or reasonably so
White, but not lily-white and usually deep-red

Thirty-fiveish, and looks it lately
Five-feet-nine and one-hundred-thirty pounds: no physique

Black hair going gray, hairline receding fast
What used to be curly, now fuzzy

Brown eyes starey under beetling brow
Mole on chin, probably will become a wen

It is perfectly obvious that he was not popular at school
No good at baseball, and wet his bed.

His aliases tell his history: Dumbell, Good-for-nothing,
Jewboy, Fieldinsky, Skinny, Fierce Face, Greaseball, Sissy.

Warning: This man is not dangerous, answers to any name
Responds to love, don't call him or he will come.

Alienation. What image does it conjure up? The
spreading, middle-aged suburban housewife with yesterday's
dreams and today's frustrations? The disgruntled businessman
with yesterday's promotion and today's stagnation? The sullen
college student with today's zealous idealism and tomorrow's
dull reality (or should we say "plastics, young man"?). Your-
self? Your friends? Your neighbors? Possibly all these people.
It seems almost fashionable to be alienated these days. And to
speak of alienation. Philosophers do. So do social scientists,
politicians, historians, and men of letters.

But when we speak of alienation what do we mean?
What *is* alienation? The word has come to stand for all the
miseries endured by man alone: his feeling of loneliness in a
hostile, foreboding world; his sense of being unknown and unwanted; in short, his experience of being *alien*ated. Alienated
man is man isolated and lonely; man estranged from himself
and his fellow man; man without meaning or direction—a
human nonbeing passing his hours in "quiet desperation." He
is, if you will, a person devoid of linkages within himself and
with the outside world. There is no connectiveness anywhere,
no attachments: he is, in essence, a human shell in a vacuum
—a void within a void.

The plight of alienated man is his inability to answer
the age-old questions: "Who am I?" "Where am I?" "Where
am I going?" He has lost his identity, his place in the world,
his sense of human destiny. He becomes—instead of Horatio
Alger, the self-made man—a Willie Loman, the selfless man.
The American, caught in the throes of alienation, identifies
with Arthur Miller's dying salesman. This is why the businessman, once a main character in the American success story,

now becomes a central figure in an American tragedy. William Shakespeare once asked: "To be or not to be?" Alienated man —in his dehumanized condition—represents a tragic answer to that question.

Man's alienation. Perhaps T. S. Eliot described it most succinctly in *The Hollow Men*.

> We are the hollow men
> We are the stuffed men
> Leaning together
> Headpiece filled with straw. Alas!
> Shape without form, shade without colour,
> Paralyzed force, feature without motion.

If one doubts the existence of alienation in our society he need only turn to American artistic, philosophical, and scientific comment over the past 70 years to discover just how long such a condition has been with us and how pervasive it is. Such a historical overview would also reveal a recent intensification of alienation in America and a corresponding increase in attention to the problem. Today there are even sourcebooks on the topic of alienation (see, for example, Burrows & Lapides, 1969; Josephson & Josephson, 1962; Marcson, 1970; Sykes, 1964)—a sure sign that the concept is widely recognized and used as one way of describing and understanding contemporary human behavior.

## The Theme of Alienation in Works of Art

Some of the earliest and most perceptive views of America's alienation came from the country's artistic community. This isn't surprising. Creative people are skilled observers and interpreters of the world in which they live—specially endowed with the acute sensitivity necessary to comprehend and express the events around them with clarity and insight.

Today more than ever before man's alienation is being explored in American art, literature, drama, cinema, and music. Consider art, for example. We have already presented Tooker's *The Subway* as one artistic portrayal of alienation. Some others are presented on the following pages. Some are pieces of sculpture, like Segal's *Old Woman at a Window* (Plate 2); others are paintings, like Wyeth's *Christina's World* (Plate 3).

Often the artist conveys alienation by portraying man as dehumanized or at the mercy of forces he cannot control. In Hirsch's *Interior with Figures* (Plate 4), the "figures" are essentially nondescript carbon copies of each other—similarly dressed, similarly acting "puppets" laboring in the shadow of "Big Brother's" sinister face. There is little to suggest individuality, individual worth, or self-determination in these figures.

Sometimes the alienation theme of an artistic work is not so readily apparent to the observer. A case in point is David Smith's sculpture *Lonesome Man* (Plate 5). The title suggests a study of alienation, but where in the lines of metal does the face of alienation lurk? In the face that observes it! If the reader were to view the Smith work in actuality he would see his image in the highly polished surface of the sculpture. When *Lonesome Man* is viewed as a mirror, its message is obvious.

## The Theme of Alienation in Scholarly Works

> *At the present time, in all the social sciences, the various synonyms of alienation have a foremost place in studies of human relations. Investigations of the "unattached," the "marginal," the "obsessive," the "normless," and the "isolated" individual all testify to the central place occupied by the hypothesis of alienation in contemporary social science.*
>
> Robert Nisbet (1953)

While members of the American artistic community were busily commenting on the developing state of alienation, American scholars were not sitting idly by. Psychologists, sociologists, and philosophers were also making statements on the subject and, like the painters, poets, and playwrights, their message was a somber reminder that man is losing his sense of self in the face of alienation.

Consider, for example, the works of "humanistic" psychologists like Erich Fromm, Abraham Maslow, Rollo May, and Carl Rogers. These professionals, many of them practicing psychotherapists, took a basically optimistic stance on the issue of human capabilities; they were convinced that man, if given the proper conditions and the opportunity, would "self-actualize"—would realize his full potential as a human being. It was this faith in personal dignity—the belief that man, in a supportive environment, could become all he was capable of becoming—that earned for the humanistic psychologist the title "The Menschmaker."

But what of people who were unable to attain self-actualization? What seemed to be their difficulty? According to the humanistic psychologist, man's alienation was the stumbling block to successful self-development. Put simply, the alienated person couldn't expect to "self-actualize" when he had no sense of self in the first place. The major task confronting modern man, then, was to find himself, to discover the meaning of life in terms of his own perspectives and orientation. His opportunity for healthy psychological growth depended on it. This emphasis on man's need to seek out his identity is reflected in the titles of books written by psychologists in the humanistic tradition: two examples are Rollo May's *Man's Search for Himself* and Virginia Axline's *Dibs: In Search of Self.*

The humanistic psychologists were not alone in considering alienation a formidable obstacle in man's quest for identity. In the writings of other psychologists (for example, Keniston's *The Uncommitted*), sociologists (Reisman's *The Lonely Crowd*), and philosophers (Marcuse's *One-Dimensional Man*) the point is clearly made: Alienation undermines personal vitality in society and lays waste to individual self-development and self-determination. As one social scientist put it: "Alienation is toxin to the human spirit."

## How Does Alienated Man Behave?

American artists and scholars have provided an invaluable service. By calling our attention to the problem of alienation in society and providing us with a description of the alienated individual, he has put us in a better position to appreciate the impact of this condition in contemporary culture and to see how it affects the course of human behavior.

How *does* alienated man behave? When poet T. S. Eliot describes him as a "hollow man" and sociologist C. Wright Mills calls him a "cheerful robot" we begin to sense the answer. It would seem that the alienated individual lacks the "ego strength" (the "self power") to become an active manipulator of his world. Instead, like a "weather vane man" controlled by the capricious whims of each passing breeze, he is manipulated by forces external to himself. How else could we expect the alienated individual to behave? Alienation guts a man of his will to act; destroys his sense of self-determination and makes him impotent in an omnipotent world. He becomes, for all practical purposes, a power vacuum lacking the internal strength to repulse the assaults of external demands. In the words of Erich Fromm, he "does not experience himself as the center of his world, as the center of his own acts—but his acts and their consequences have become his masters, whom he obeys, or whom he may even worship."

In his powerless state, alienated man usually responds by (1) rigorously following the directives of others, depending on them for guidance and rules of conduct, or (2) rejecting others in favor of a "loner's" existence. The alienated individual who follows the first course of action gains a certain stability and sense of direction at the cost of his self-determination. Self-reliance is sacrificed in favor of other-reliance; individual initiative is replaced by the initiative of others. Pursuit of the second course of action gives the person a certain sense of autonomy, but it is a negative autonomy—one leading to anomie, isolation, and loneliness. Alienated loners often lead disorganized lives, lives without unifying themes or purposes—helter-skelter lives where they experience, according to Keniston, "an intense feeling of the precariousness and diversity of the self, . . . doubt about their own continuing capacity to 'cope,' coupled with a relentless search for some trustworthy foundation for selfhood" (Keniston, 1960). Few ever find the selfhood they so desperately seek.

In contemporary America the tragic results of prolonged alienation are apparent. One sees them in New York City, where a 16-year-old boy is found dead of a heroin overdose; in San Francisco, where a 17-year-old grants sexual favors to any willing rock musician; in Atlanta, where a middle-aged married man with two children leaves his job and family to join a commune; and in Chicago, where an elderly lady roams the streets searching for visitors from outer space. One senses in these people, by their actions, a desperate feeling of emptiness; a driving need to fill their personal void; a frantic search for something to put their faith in. It is little wonder that General Motors describes its Buick motor car as "something to believe in"; or that Standard Oil presents "I'm a believer" buttons to converts willing to swear by its better-mileage gasoline. To the alienated American, believing in cars and gasoline is better than believing in nothing at all.

Who knows—maybe Madison Avenue will give man the faith and substance he needs to overcome his alienation. Maybe, though we doubt it. Of this, however, there is no doubt: until man finds himself we will continue to encounter confused, unhappy Americans or, possibly more frightening, Americans who are totally subservient to the dictates of others.

# THE ALIENATED AMERICAN AND THE SPECTER OF PSYTOCRACY

**5**

> *The serious threat to our democracy is not
> existence of foreign totalitarian states. It is
> the existence within our own personal
> attitudes and within our own institutions
> of conditions which have given a victory to
> external authority, discipline, uniformity
> and dependence. . . . The battlefield is also
> accordingly here—within ourselves and
> our institutions.*
>
> John Dewey
> *Freedom and Culture*

In the previous chapter we examined the condition of the twentieth century American. Using materials from artistic and scientific sources we sketched a tragic picture of man losing his humanity—of man hapless, helpless, and hopeless; of man estranged and dehumanized to the point of alienation.

Yet to identify the current psychological condition of man is not enough. No matter how accurate one might be in characterizing the individual as alienated, his work remains unfinished. He must also ask: "Why is man this way?" "What produces his alienation?" Such a line of inquiry is vitally needed. By discovering the cause of alienation we edge closer to discovering its cure.

## How Did Twentieth Century Americans Become Alienated?

Getting to the root of alienation in modern man is like trying to uncover the basis of a lover's devotion. Many factors contribute to the "condition"—so many, in fact, that an exhaustive answer is impossible. However, certain major determinants in the alienation experience can be identified, one of which we will discuss at length here. We refer to the growth of the *Szeitgeist* and its impact on man's conception of himself as a free entity. As we shall see, the Szeitgeist in America is intimately bound up with the psychological condition of its citizens.

### What Is the Szeitgeist?

You won't find the definition of Szeitgeist in a dictionary. Like "psytocracy," it is a neologism—a word we created to express an idea difficult to communicate with standard terms. Szeitgeist is formed from combining the English word *science* with the German word *Zeitgeist* (literally: "spirit of the time"), to arrive at the meaning: *the scientific spirit of the times*.

Why the necessity for this new word? We will be arguing that the meteoric rise of science in the twentieth century has had a telling impact on man, undermining his spirit of freedom and making him feel selfless and alienated. But do we really mean that *science* has had this impact? Is science some form of purposeful, antidemocratic tyrant pledged to the extermination of man's self-determination? Of course not! Science is a way of looking at the world; a procedure for asking and answering questions; a body of data collected by orderly, controlled procedures. Yet the products and philosophy of science do influence man—of this there is no doubt. In space-age jargon, there are "spin-offs" from science. The discovery of the atom, the creation of computers, the production of polio vaccine—all these events modify the lives of men and the world they inhabit. We live today, more than ever before, in an age shaped by science. At every turn we experience the results of scientific endeavor: in our technology and our religion; in our schools and our leisure; in the way we think and the way we live. But—and this is important—it is not science per se that shapes the minds of men. Such a definition is too narrow. Rather, man is influenced by the *scientific spirit of the times*—that particular philosophical and technological social milieu that is born of, but is greater than, science itself.

## Man: Bent, Folded, and Mutilated

When most of us think of science we think of moonshots and missiles; computers, and condensers. What we often fail to think about is the intellectual and emotional impact such scientific innovations have: how discoveries in science bring about corresponding discoveries in the way we see ourselves and our role in society. For example, LSD represents, in one sense, a scientific discovery—the detection of a powerful mind-altering substance; yet, in a second sense, it is more, far more—the catalytic agent in man's changing conception of himself and his world. Some people make the distinction this way: the discovery of LSD is a scientific revelation; the impact of LSD on man is a psychedelic revolution.

Garvin McCain and Erwin Segal further illustrate how discoveries in science can influence a person's self-conception in their delightful book, *The Game of Science*.

> Science affects belief. . . . For example, when Copernicus and Galileo shattered the earth's pretensions as the center of the physical universe, the impact was much greater than the astro-

nomical consequences of accepting the sun as the center of the universe. Presumably, the Copernican concept of the universe did not change the productivity of the fields, turn wine to vinegar, or render less fascinating the pursuit of women and war. And yet, when a long established and firmly held belief is shattered, life can never be the same (McCain & Segal, 1969).

In what ways has the Szeitgeist undermined man's spirit of freedom and led to his self-estrangement and alienation? By damaging his ego, his sense of direction, his stability, his dignity as a human being and his faith in survival. Let us examine each of these effects separately.

## The Szeitgeist and Man's Ego

Before the Renaissance one could hardly blame man for being egotistical. Unique among God's creatures, blessed with the power of reason and thought, he ruled the Earth when Earth ruled the universe! Of such knowledge is self-pride and self-respect built.

Then along came Copernicus. This upstart astronomer had the guile to suggest that the Earth was not the center of the universe. Unfortunately for man's self-conception, he also had the proof to back up his claims. The Copernican doctrine was a body-blow to man's ego. It displaced him as the center of the universe, but at least he was still the center of his planet . . . or was he?

Hardly had man steadied himself from this ego-pummeling at the hands of Copernicus when Charles Darwin arrived to deliver a second well-aimed blow. Copernicus had challenged man's position in space; Darwin challenged his position on earth. That was hitting close to home!

Prior to Darwin man had envisioned himself as a unique form of life on his planet. After all, what animal had a soul?

To suggest otherwise was to invite amusement, indignation, or wrath, depending on the physical stature of the listener. Yet, Darwin made just such a suggestion—and in tones loud enough to shake church and state. To Darwin man was brighter and more adaptive than other animals—but the difference was quantitative rather than qualitative; an issue of degree, not of kind. Man remained an animal, albeit a highly developed one. Once-proud man, relegated to a corner of the universe, was now related to his animal ancestors. It wasn't a happy family reunion.

If Copernicus and Darwin delivered a one-two punch to man's ego, then it became Freud's privilege to try to administer the *coup de grâce*. Like Copernicus and Darwin, Freud was a renegade in his own time—an individual who challenged and changed men's conceptions. By assaulting the rationality of man in an era that stressed human reason and understanding, Freud stood as a colossus in the changing thought currents of Western civilization. His belief that human behavior was often motivated and determined by unconscious thought processes was a bitter pill for twentieth century man to swallow. Deposed from his celestial hub and linked with vine-swinging apes, he was now told he lacked control over his own mind. "Your mind is like an iceberg," Freud said in effect. "The smallest part, the part containing your conscious thoughts, lies within your view. The greatest mass, however—the unconscious—remains below the surface of your awareness." Man, in other words, couldn't even be sure of his own thoughts.

One university professor, pondering the fate of man's shrinking ego in the face of scientific assault, summarized it this way: with Copernicus man lost his throne; with Darwin he lost his soul; and with Freud he lost his mind.

Is there anything left of man's ego? Yes, but not much. Not only has he been stripped of belief in his own centrality, spirituality, and rationality; he has yet to find a new set of

ego-strengthening beliefs to take their place. Possibly the con-
quest of space will instill in man a new self-pride that comes
with conquering the unknown. But even if this "shot in the
ego" does occur it might be offset by scientific progress in
areas that reduce man's sense of self (for example, the production of test-tube babies or of robots that outperform humans).

Of one thing we can be certain: the Szeitgeist has, over
the past three centuries, forced man to make major devalua-
tions in his self-worth. We believe such profound ego adjust-
ments have played a role in man's growing sense of alienation.
Unless the individual finds a new set of convictions to revital-
ize his self-image, the next blow to his ego might well be the
knockout punch.

## The Szeitgeist and Man's Sense of Direction

Just as man's sense of ego has been weakened in the scientific spirit of the times, so has his sense of direction. Man
has lost faith in his capacity to know where he's going, and at
the same time, he has lost the feelings of security that accom-
pany this faith. Faced with such uncertainty, the individual
has become unsure of his world, his beliefs, his future, himself.

Before the scientific revolution man had about as much
direction as he could possibly want. Religion gave him a life
plan and theologians were quite willing to help him follow it.
There was an overriding sense of surety in the churchgoer's
life—after all, there isn't much uncertainty in a heaven-or-hell
alternative, especially when the procedures for getting to each
place are known.

The Szeitgeist buckled the credibility of the religious establishment in the eyes of many of the faithful. The sense of
direction that religious doctrine had provided dissipated as
the validity of ecclesiastical tenets were challenged on scientific
grounds. Some people continued to cling tenaciously to

church values for guidance, but the power of theology to provide man with a sense of direction would never be the same.

The most tragic aspect of the church crisis was this: as religion lost its stabilizing force in man's life, nothing as effective took its place. Man had once looked to God for direction; now where could he look? Many people turned to science for guidance. Science, which had taken the edge off religion, became a religion in its own right. It was worshiped, extolled, praised as a way of life. Particularly in the eighteenth and nineteenth centuries the scientific spirit of the times seemed to give great numbers of people the stability they had once experienced in the church. The universe seemed orderly and open to understanding; science was entrusted to uncover its secrets. In the new religion research replaced reverence; technology replaced theology; and probing replaced praying. God was still God, but Newton was the new Pope.

By the twentieth century, however, it was obvious that science, at least in the foreseeable future, would not provide man with the same degree of direction he had found in religion. This realization was based, in large part, on a change in scientific thinking. Whereas earlier generations of scientists had been confident of achieving certainty of knowledge in their work, twentieth century scientists rejected such an idea. It was becoming increasingly apparent that science didn't have exact answers, and might never have them. The evolving language of science reflected this change in opinion. Terms like "mechanistic" and "deterministic" were being replaced by "relativistic" and "probabilistic." Even the Pope was replaced! Now the likes of Einstein and Heisenberg handed down dictums where once Newton's canons were law.

It is not surprising that modern man, deprived of his religious security by a science that could not replace it, has experienced an intensifying alienation. Caught between deity and decimal—not totally satisfied with either—the twentieth century American has been set adrift in a sea of uncertainty with no sense of direction to steer a course homeward.

## The Szeitgeist and Man's Sense of Stability

Although we might be accused of historical egocentrism, we feel justified in claiming that contemporary Americans live in the most rapidly changing world that has ever existed. Allen Wheelis describes this state of affairs aptly in *The Quest for Identity:*

> Now, for perhaps the first time in his life on earth, man is obliged to adjust, not simply to changed conditions, but to change itself. In the past he had to give up the old and adapt to the new; now he must adapt, also, to the certain knowledge that the new, with unprecedented rapidity, is being replaced by that which is to follow. Before he becomes fully acquainted with the emerging circumstances of life he is distracted by the moving shadows of their unknown successors. As a modern aircraft may be obsolete by the time it comes off the production line, so the conditions of man's life begin to pass away before he has fairly come to grips with them (Wheelis, 1958).

The impact of this accelerating rate of change on man has been, of course, monumental. In earlier times man, society, the world moved at a more leisurely pace. Progress was gradual; adjustment relatively simple. Recently all this has been altered. With the forward thrust of science and technology man has confronted an ever-accelerating panorama of change—breath-taking reorganizations of life that have left him struggling to keep pace with his discoveries. This relentless advance has cost man his stability, and it threatens his sanity—particularly in America, where he is expected to find his own answers and is free to define and carve out his own place in life. It is not easy to clarify one's existence in a constantly changing world; to cope with the complexities of an always novel environment; to adapt to every new situation.

Bob Dylan was at his prophetic best when he wrote

"The times they are a-changin'." Like a train gathering speed as it clears the station yard, the tempo of alteration in our nation quickens, gathering ever more momentum. Yesterday flux and uncertainty were a part of life; today they are a way of life. Yesterday man introduced his children to the world; today they introduce him.

The Szeitgeist is intimately bound up with the pace and type of change occurring in America. Science and technology have played the leading roles in the production of change in this country, and they will continue to do so. Man's current difficulties occur because he creates scientific products faster than he constructs rules for governing their use. (To create an atom bomb is one thing; to live with it quite another!) In other words, man's cultural innovations haven't kept pace with his innovations in science: he hasn't developed the guidelines (institutions) for living in the world he has created! Take the problem of longevity. Progress in medicine has helped us keep people alive longer; yet our cultural institutions have lagged behind medical advances, and now that we have senior citizens we don't know what to do with them.

The gap between the institutions of society and the innovations of science has much to do with man's current state of alienation. The citizen is swamped in the scientific spirit of his time; he has no cultural directives for coping with the technological innovations that confront him.

Anthropologists speak of "culture shock." Culture shock occurs when members of a culture are confronted by an innovation so prodigious that it "blows their minds." The term *culture shock* is usually reserved for the reactions encountered in a primitive culture when its population is introduced to advanced technological implements, such as guns or heavy machinery. We venture to suggest that America is the only nation we know of that can generate its own culture shock! And, we further suggest, as long as American science continues to produce ideas and implements that boggle the minds of most American citizens we will have many unstabilized, alienated individuals in our society.[11]

## The Szeitgeist and Man's Dehumanization

To dehumanize a man you strip him of his dignity, his sense of self, his feeling of worth, his faith that he can change the world in which he lives. There is something very dehumanizing about the experience shown in Lorenz's cartoon (Plate 6). Is it the revulsion we feel when we see man at the mercy of a machine? Does the cartoon remind us of the vending machine that took our dime but refused us food? The radar trap that caught us speeding? The huge pressing machine that deprived us of our job? Yes, all these things and more. The drawing captures the confrontation of human man and inhuman machine—the struggle to determine who shall rule, man or machine. This confrontation has taken on new importance in the age of computers and, we will argue, has relevance for contemporary man's feelings of alienation and personal devaluation.

The dehumanization of man by machine is not a product of twentieth century America. During the Industrial Revolution in England, when machine technology came of age, mechanical devices were blamed for the demise of the worker's dignity and feeling of worth. Then, as now, the machine presents a paradox: built to serve man it is often accused of enslaving him. Sometimes this slavery is physical—workers are in a sense "chained fast to the iron machine." Other times the slavery is psychological—the individual is intimidated by machines and comes to see himself as helpless before them. By such perceptions is dehumanization produced. Bruno Bettelheim reports a case study of a little boy, Joey, who believed he was a machine. When asked to draw his self-portrait, Joey sketched a "machine man"—his own self-image in a machine age. Such a self-perception illustrates the impact of machine technology on the human spirit.

Although the dehumanization of man by machine did not originate in America, it has reached its most intense form here. Why? Because the United States is the first country to progress from industrial to electronic revolution; from "brawn machines" to "brain machines." The computer has become a twentieth century American institution. With its ascendancy man has had to defend his worth against machines that can reason as well as work. Such a defense has not been easy. To confront a machine that can outwork a man is a formidable, but not overwhelming, challenge. After all, horses can pull heavier loads than men. But in the face of an apparatus spawned by IBM, imposing in size and expense, and able to perform tasks previously reserved exclusively for human intellect—then man's defense of his worth is difficult indeed. Horses might pull heavy cargo but they don't plot orbits for lunar space probes!

The psychological impact of computers on man—their contribution to his dehumanization—should not be underestimated. The computer, by performing superhuman feats, has caused man to perceive himself as subhuman by comparison. Knowing that the computer is controlled by human directives might offer consolation to a few thousand computer programmers, but to the millions of people who are outthought, outmaneuvered, and outmoded by the "electronic monolith," it does not. The computer has taken on an aura of omnipotence in our society: it is an authority beyond challenge because it is beyond human foibles. It has become, in a sense, the new God for the new times—an electronic deity in the scientific spirit of the times. Or, perhaps, the new devil.

The dehumanization of man. The computer is not the only culprit responsible for the current state of affairs. The philosopher of science also plays a role when he takes the position that human behavior can be controlled. To the man in the street, already eclipsed by the computer, it is not very uplifting to be told that science is out to control his behavior. That such control might be used for man's benefit (for example, to cure disease) doesn't seem to offset the dehumanizing realization by the individual that his own actions are "open game" for scientific scrutiny and manipulation. As long as scientific philosophy presents the control of behavior as basic to scientific activity, many people will feel alienated in the face of scientific progress.


## The Szeitgeist and Man's Faith in Survival

One need only recall the Cuban missile crisis to be reminded that the fear of mass extermination in a nuclear age is a part of us all. While American and Russian naval forces played out their exercise in brinksmanship on the high seas, John Q. Public huddled near his radio or TV, feeling increasingly helpless and desperate in the face of possible annihilation. When the Russian ships turned away from Cuba there was an almost euphoric sense of national relief—the elation that comes when a momentous tragedy is averted. Yet, while the specter of nuclear holocaust seemed imminent, people were paralyzed from a sense of dread and the realization that they could not control their own destiny. Is it any wonder some of them felt alienated?

Today, with the continuation of the cold war, the creation of ever more powerful doomsday weapons, and the proliferation of nuclear armaments, all men live perpetually on death row. Ours is the age of the *nuclear psychosis,* a time when man's faith in long-term survival is challenged by his day-to-day confrontation with the bomb. It is interesting to note that today's American youth—possibly the most alienated generation ever to live in our country—are the first Americans to grow up with the full realization of what the nuclear age truly means for human survival.

Man is a forward-looking creature. Much of his sense of self comes from developing and accomplishing long-term life goals. As long as the conditions of today threaten the chances of tomorrow, the state of alienation will remain a prominent feature of contemporary American life.

## Does Alienated Man Desire Psytocracy?

As we pointed out in Chapter 3, behavior control can be used to further the cause of democracy *or* of psytocracy—to liberate or to subjugate man, to free or to enslave him. And the condition of man is an important determinant of how behavior control will be used. To the person who values freedom and can live comfortably with it, behavior control can be a most valued means of sustaining self-determination and individual initiative. But to those who find freedom overwhelming, it would curtail choice and develop a dependency on others.

At the risk of sounding blasphemous, we would suggest that the average American citizen today (unknowingly and unwittingly) is one of democracy's most underrated and formidable foes. In his alienated state, the twentieth century American is unequal to the challenges of twentieth century democracy: he is unable to live and grow, survive, and flourish, in the society he venerates. Stated simply, he cannot exist comfortably in a democratic political system because he cannot cope with the freedom it provides. The United States citizen is a democrat at heart but not in mind. He has learned to love freedom, but not to live it; he has been told freedom exists but is not trained to cope with it.

Why is this so? Because the contemporary American, caught in a crisis of self, has steadily, inexorably, lost faith in his own capacity to be free, to make his mark upon the world, to be active rather than reactive.

To be free one must believe he is free. He must believe that by his actions he can, in some ways, control the outcome of his own destiny. Further, he must be willing to exercise his right to act in achieving his goals. The truly free individual must have a sense of "internal causation," a sense that he is more than a passive entity at the mercy of the "slings and arrows of outrageous fortune." He must perceive himself as a causal agent—an organism capable of acting upon his environment: changing, shaping, manipulating it. Innovation and individual initiative are expected of the free man—for, in a society where decisions are not made for him, he must be willing and able to make his own way in life.

Our alienated American certainly doesn't make much of a causal agent! How does a "hollow man" adjust to a situation where he is expected to find his own answers to problems and is free to define and carve out his own place in life? Oftentimes he doesn't. One important reason for the lack of public opposition to our increasingly organizational democracy is the important advantage it offers the harassed American: it absolves him of many personal responsibilities. An organizational democracy is willing to tell a person what to do and how to do it, to provide for him a niche or a role that he can occupy or follow in effortless conformity.

In the case of alienated man, freedom is not enough. Or perhaps we should say it is too much. In his alienated condition the individual finds himself overwhelmed by freedom— somewhat like a eunuch thrust into a sheik's harem. Unprepared to keep pace with a constantly changing world, stripped of his ego by a science he reveres, dehumanized in a society where his identity resides on a piece of computer tape, unsure of his chances for long-term survival, unpracticed in self-determination, and facing the awesome responsibility of free choice —is it any wonder that the United States citizen seeks an escape from freedom or, equally as tragic, is dissatisfied with being free?

The idea that alienated man would voluntarily reject democratic traditions is brilliantly expounded by Erich Fromm in his classic work, *Escape from Freedom*. Taking an "out of the frying pan into the fire" approach, Fromm sees the alienated individual released from one form of control only to face another. Emphasizing the importance of man's selfhood in the quest for a meaningful personal freedom, Fromm warns us that:

Freedom has a twofold meaning for modern man: that he has been freed from traditional authorities and has become an "individual," but that at the same time he has become isolated, powerless, and an instrument of purposes outside of himself, alienated from himself and others; furthermore, that this state undermines his self, weakens and frightens him, and makes him ready for submission to new kinds of bondage. . . . Man does not suffer so much from poverty today as he suffers from the fact that he has become a cog in a large machine, an automaton, that his life has become empty and lost its meaning. . . . Democracy . . . will triumph over the forces of nihilism only if it can imbue people with a faith that is the strongest the human mind is capable of, the faith in life and in truth, and in freedom as the active and spontaneous realization of the individual self (Fromm, 1941).

Like Fromm, we believe that alienated man is in danger of losing his freedom unless he finds himself. We feel that, in his present condition, the average American is becoming ever more susceptible to (or should we say desirous of) psytocracy. When science finds new ways to control human behavior and the individual abrogates his rights as a free man in favor of control by others who use the new regulatory methods to circumscribe his liberties, then democracy is in grave danger. Man must want freedom to have it. Democratic apathy—the voluntary denial of self-determination—is the most insidious and formidable foe of a free society—a fifth column far more destructive to democratic institutions than the pillages of war and political intrigues. When the individual seeks to limit his "inalienable rights" of freedom, the Declaration of Independence and the Bill of Rights seem a bit less indestructible. C. Wright Mills recognizes the danger of the current American malaise when he points out that "the alienated man is the antithesis of the Western image of the free man. The society in which this man, this cheerful robot, flourishes is the antithesis of the free society—or in the literal and plain meaning of the word, of a democratic society."

*Plate 1.* George Tooker. *The Subway.* 1950. Egg tempera on composition board. 18⅛ × 36⅛". Collection of Whitney Museum of American Art, New York (Juliana Force Purchase).

*Plate 2.* George Segal. *Old Woman at a Window.* 1965. Plaster, chrome, wood, glass, and board, 96×36×48″. Collection Mr. and Mrs. Melvin Hirsh, Beverly Hills, California. Courtesy Sidney Janis Gallery, New York.

*Plate 3.* Andrew Wyeth. *Christina's World.* 1948. Tempera on gesso panel, 32¼ × 47¾". Collection, Museum of Modern Art, New York.

*Plate 4.* Joseph Hirsch. *Interior with Figures.* 1962. Oil on canvas, 45×72″. Whitney Museum of American Art, New York (gift of Mr. and Mrs. Daniel Fraad, Jr.).

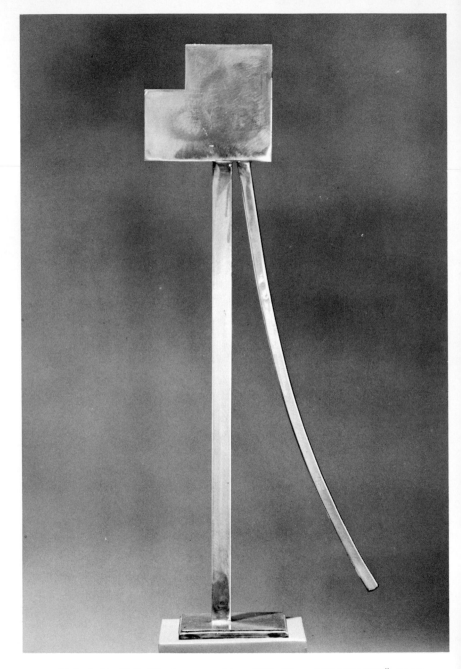

*Plate 5.* David Smith. *Lonesome Man.* 1957. Silver, $27\frac{1}{2} \times 9\frac{1}{2} \times \frac{1}{2}''$. Estate of the artist, courtesy Marlborough-Gerson Gallery.

*"Down!"*

*Plate 6.* Drawing by Lorenz; © 1961 *The New Yorker Magazine, Inc.*

## An American Dilemma

The condition of twentieth century American science and that of twentieth century American man have brought us to a critical point. For the first time science is on the verge of creating an effective behavior control technology, but man's alienation makes him most susceptible to using that technology to develop a psytocracy. When such conditions appear together we have the following equation:

$$\begin{array}{c} \text{Effective behavior} \\ \text{control technology} \end{array} + \begin{array}{c} \text{Alienated} \\ \text{individuals} \end{array} = \begin{array}{c} \text{Conditions conducive} \\ \text{to formation of a} \\ \text{psytocracy} \end{array}$$

If there is hope of arresting man's drift toward psytocracy—if there is a way we can buttress his faith in democratic processes—it seems to lie in reversing the course of alienation in our society, in starting our citizens back on the road to selfhood. The way back will not be easy.

# 6 PUTTING MAN DOWN AND BUILDING MAN UP

*What a piece of work is man! How noble
in reason! how infinite in faculties! in form
and moving, how express and admirable!
in action, how like an angel! in apprehension,
how like a god! the beauty of the world! the
paragon of animals! And yet, to me, what is
this quintessence of dust?*
                    Hamlet
                    Act II, Scene II

*Since all the faculties of the soul depend to
such a degree on the proper organization
of the brain, . . . the soul is clearly an
enlightened machine.*
                    La Mettrie
                    *L'Homme machine* (1748)

We began this book (Chapter 1) by describing some of the advances in behavior control technology that put man on the threshold of regulating his own psychosocial evolution. After taking issue with three common misconceptions about behavior control (Chapter 2), we outlined two visions of American sociopolitical organization (Chapter 3) and emphasized that behavior control could be used to facilitate and accelerate either trend.

We then speculated on the direction in which society would move: toward *participatory democracy* with its emphasis on human individuality and initiative or toward *psytocracy* with its emphasis on human conformity and passivity. We argued that the *alienated* condition of twentieth century American (Chapter 4 and 5) enhances the likelihood of psytocracy.

At the end of the preceding chapter we expressed our belief that the best hope for halting man's drift toward psytocracy seems to lie in reversing the course of alienation in our society, in starting our citizens back on the road to selfhood. This will involve instilling in man a new sense of himself, putting some self-polish on his tarnished image, showing him he has the potential to be a unique, dignified, full, *autonomous* human being.

Self-esteem (self-worth) has long been recognized as a motivating force in man by Western philosophers, particularly Adam Smith, David Hume, Auguste Kant, and Jean Jacques Rousseau. Kant wrote, "A craving to inspire in others esteem for ourselves through good behavior . . . is the basis of true sociality." When man has a high opinion of himself and his abilities he is likely to lead a richer, more productive, and more fulfilling life. This is one of the reasons why many psychologists and psychiatrists are turning from analysis to therapy in treating their patients. The danger of analysis is that people come to see themselves as hopelessly determined by events, while therapy tries to elevate the individual's self-concept.

We cannot overemphasize the importance of man's self-concept in determining the future direction of American social organization. If each man sees himself as nothing more than a simple reflex organism—a dim, flickering light in the universal pinball machine—then a psytocracy is inevitable. If, however, the potential of modern man has been underestimated— if he has the potential to be free—then there is hope. We turn now to an examination of man's self-concept and, finally, back to the subject of our first chapter, behavioral science, this time to discover not how man can be controlled, but what man is capable of being.

## The Importance of Feeling Free

A belief in personal freedom is central to psychological health. Even in the supremely fatalistic Islamic cultures, people retain a feeling of autonomy. Psychologist Ludwig Immergluck (1964) observes, "Our self image, such as it is, and such as it has possibly evolved in all human cultures, appears to demand at least some feeling of inner spontaneity, a psychological conviction that one is not helplessly entrapped by circumstances, past and present, and that one can, after all is said and done, transcend one's own determining confines." *The problem with alienated man is that he has lost faith in his generative powers.* As his self-image diminishes, he becomes an increasingly willing and vulnerable victim of a psytocracy. Unfortunately, the declining process is self-perpetuating. The less free man feels, the less free he acts; the less free he acts, the less free he feels; and so on. In the words of Keniston (1960):

> A characteristic conviction of many modern men and women is the . . . deterministic sense of being caught in a psychosocial vise, locked so tightly it cannot be loosened without destroying it altogether. As a consequence, we dare change nothing at all.

Recognizing that Americans need a sense of freedom to combat alienation is one thing; giving them the means to experience that freedom in their own lives is quite another! The difficulty of the task is intensified by religious and scientific doctrines that challenge freedom either by ignoring it or underestimating man's potential to possess it.

## Three Strikes Against Freedom

Three strikes and you're out. In many intellectual ball parks the freedom team isn't even allowed to play. For example, in his latest book, *Love and Will,* Rollo May describes the pathetic situation of many practicing psychiatrists who simultaneously help their patients to rediscover personal freedom yet privately deny that anything approaching it even exists. Why is freedom out of the game? Strike one is grounded in ecclesiastical traditions that have influenced alienated man's attitude toward "free choice" in a subtle but profound manner. The religious influence dates back to the ascendancy of Judaism and Christianity, which fragmented the unified study of man into two parts: [12] the behavioral sciences, which were concerned with bodily mechanics, and theology, which dealt with the interaction of mind and soul. This distinction began with Philo of Alexandria (c. 30 A.D.), who tried to unite Greek psychology with Hebrew theism, declaring that the purpose of life is to restore the "fallen soul" by understanding and disciplining the body. "O, my soul," he writes, "travel through the land and through man, bringing, if you think fit, each individual man to a judgment of the things which concern him; as for instance, what the body is and under what influences, whether active or passive, it cooperates with the mind" (quoted in Brett, 1912). The separation of human behavior into two distinct provinces was crystallized by Saint Augustine, who recognized "how many things we share in common not only with the animals but also with the trees and plants, for we observe that bodily nutrition, growth, reproduction, and health are also proper to trees, which make up the lowest level of life" [Augustinus (translated by Russell), 1968]. To separate man from the "baser" creatures, Augustine endowed him with a "free and independent" soul, which possesses the qualities of freedom and responsibility. According to Augustine, the soul is imparted to the body by the breath of God at the time of birth.

The positive consequences of dividing man into body and soul are well known to historians of behavioral science. When Descartes located the soul in the pineal gland at the front of the brain (c. 1650), he freed scientists to explore the *machinery* of animals and of the remainder of the human body without danger of violating religious precepts. However, the negative consequences of this division have never been fully appreciated. During the 12 centuries that separated Augustine from Descartes, a belief in free choice became inextricably confused with the concept of soul. A refutation of one automatically implied a refutation of the other. The result is that, as scientists eliminated the need for a soul as an explanatory concept in behavioral science, *the belief in free choice was simultaneously eliminated.* Instead of extending behavioral science to account for the complex human actions of choice and creativity, investigators dismissed them as either nonexistent or illusory. Even worse, the scientists who continued to believe in freedom were similarly imbued with the notion that freedom must exist outside science. They temporarily salvaged freedom by incorporating it into the ancient doctrine of *vitalism,* which held that living organisms are not strictly determined and operate according to principles that transcend science. But, in the long run, this metaphysical maneuver only further alienated science from freedom. When vitalism was finally discredited in the mid-nineteenth century by German chemist Friedrich Wöhler, who synthesized an organic compound from inorganic materials, scientists permanently classified freedom, along with the soul, as an ancient and outmoded doctrine.

The traditional association of freedom with the metaphysics of soul and the vital principle has seriously damaged modern man's conception of his own autonomy. Science's refutation of metaphysics is a simultaneous refutation of human freedom. Today, people tacitly assume that *freedom* and *determinism* are incompatible, that these words necessarily belong to separate vocabularies, and that any discussion of freedom is outside the realm of scientific thought. Hence, the following statement by Freud makes perfect sense to scientists and laymen alike: "The deeply rooted belief in psychic freedom and choice must give way before claims of determinism which govern mental life." Modern man is virtually blind to the possibilities of affirming his autonomy within the framework of science.

Strike two: if alienated man has been deprived of freedom by the decline of the soul, his deprivation is made more acute by his belief that he is a simplistic organism—a belief grounded in a distorted view of behavioral science. Research on man's behavior actually covers a broad range of rich and complicated human activities, including perception, attitude formation, and communication. Unfortunately, the three areas of behavioral science that most interest the public—psychopathology, psychological testing, and behavior control—are often popularized in a way that emphasizes the limitations of human experience and complexity. The result is that alienated man's self-image, as reflected in the popular science forums of the mass media, is extremely oversimplified.

Consider how man must perceive himself when he reads popularized explanations of mental disorders—accounts supposedly reflecting current thinking in the behavioral sciences. How much freedom can he believe he possesses when abnormal behavior is diagnosed, treated, and explained in the most simplistic, cookbook fashion? With psychopathological activity presented in such a manner, one gets the impression that *all* human actions follow a few set patterns. It seems that every mother has read enough "pop" Freud to make superficial analyses of her own children (and husband, if necessary). And what college freshman doesn't love to charm his date with excerpts from *Everyday Psychoanalysis,* or some such book? The fact that *id, ego,* and *superego* are grossly simplified, artificial constructs rarely occurs to the lay reader. He goes on thinking that his own, and his neighbors' behavior is simple in form and simple to know. Human freedom pays a high price for that misconception!

Psychological testing similarly restricts the popular conception of human potential by giving the impression that individuals must fall into one of several neatly defined categories. In reality, tests are very limited tools. They are designed to compare individuals on the basis of abstract statistical averages and are useful for making specific statements about a person only when a good deal of other information about him is available. Unfortunately, testing has been abused, particularly by newspapers and magazines that feature "quickie" personality inventories such as *What Kind of Man (Woman) Are You?* or *What Type of Man (Woman) Is Best for You?* Predictably, this exploitation of psychology leaves readers with the impression that a personality can be blueprinted with 10 pencil checks on a score card.

Popularized views of psychopathology and psychological testing challenge man's sense of freedom because they make him out to be an easily understood, simple-functioning organism. The public's perceptions of behavior control lead to the same attitude of "I can't be free." In Chapter 2 we discussed Americans' fear of behavior control technology:—the belief that superscientists could manipulate every citizen's every move. This fear is indicative of the fact that behavior control experiments are reported in such a way as to stress the simplicity of human behavior, suggesting that it would be relatively easy for a few men to control every citizen's every move. Media science writers rarely point out that experiments on both animals and men are carried out under highly specific conditions (which might never exist in the "real world"), and that, even so, the behavior of subjects is often amazingly variable.

The simple mechanistic picture of man as presented in popular behavioral science literature is strengthened by casual exposure to a dehumanizing scientific jargon. (This is not a criticism of behavioral science, but simply an observation.) When alienated man turns to the behavioral sciences for affirmation of his freedom what does he discover? That man is not a person; he is an *organism*. He does not think; he makes *verbal responses*. His sacred symbols—the cross, the flag, the dove —are *visual stimuli*. The language of "pop" zoology contributes to alienated man's despair by explaining fundamental human actions with analogies to caged animals or herds of wild beasts. Imagine how Shakespeare's "what a piece of work is man . . ." might be translated into the language of behavioral science:

> Man is a complex organism, capable of many sensory discriminations. His physique allows him to adapt to a variety of circumstances; he is capable of manipulating the materials of his environment more efficiently than other animals. By these criteria, he is highest on the phylogenetic scale.

Hardly a tonic for alienation!

And strike three: Freedom is also harmed by behavioral scientists themselves when they underestimate human potential and devise experiments that preclude any chance for man to express his higher mental abilities.

The origins of this scientific practice date back to the eloquent Dr. Watson and the legacy of behaviorism. Watson was interested in the control of behavior and more: he also dearly wanted to establish psychology as an exact science. He believed that psychology had failed "signally to take its place in the world as an undisputed natural science." His solution was to throw out any references to mind or internal thought processes and to regard man as simply a stimulus-response machine. In 1913, he published his ideas under the title, "Psychology as the Behaviorist Views It":

> Psychology as the behaviorist views it is a purely objective experimental branch of natural science. Its theoretical goal is the prediction and control of behavior. Introspection forms no essential part of its methods, nor is the scientific value of its data dependent upon the readiness with which they lend themselves to interpretation in terms of consciousness. The behaviorist, in his efforts to get a unitary scheme of animal response, recognizes no dividing line between man and brute.

The behavior of man, with all its refinements and complexity, forms only a part of the behaviorist's total scheme of investigation.

Because words like *freedom* and *choice* smacked of mentalism, Watson did not even want to hear them. He equated such ideas with "voodooism." [13]

Behaviorism had a profound effect on the way psychologists approached the study of human behavior, and it has crippled the study of freedom to this day. Any attempt to deal with mental processes was branded as spurious. Behaviorism was more than another school of scientific psychology; it succeeded in masquerading as the *only* school of scientific psychology, thus exacting compliance with antimentalism from every psychologist who envied the status of the "hard scientists"—the physicists and chemists. Even in Watson's day freedom had potential champions from other areas of psychology, particularly from the German *Gestalt* experimenters, who studied the organizing functions of the mind, and from the American *functionalists,* like John Dewey, who stressed the importance of selection and thought as adaptive mechanisms. Unfortunately, the desire to seem scientific within the limited framework of mental reductionism was too strong for most experimenters to resist. Gestalt psychologists tried whenever possible to paraphrase their literature in the terminology of stimulus-response; and functionalists either conformed to behaviorism or were banished from psychology departments and relegated to less prestigious schools of education.

Only now that the technology of behavior control has established the status of psychology as a "real" science does its membership feel secure enough to acknowledge some of behaviorism's shortcomings. However, prejudice against those who study complex human mental processes persists, even in light of recent discoveries that make the necessity of such work obvious. It is reflected in current psychological jargon, which calls physiological and animal research the "hard side" of psychology, and personality and clinical study the "soft side."

## Salvaging Freedom

> *I believe that the real impact of psychology
> will be felt, not through the technological
> products it places in the hands of powerful
> men, but through its effects on the public
> at large, through a new and different public
> conception of what is humanly possible and
> what is humanly desirable.*
>
> George A. Miller
> President
> American Psychological
> Association

Many conscientious behavioral scientists hold themselves
directly responsible for the alienation of man in general, and
for the demise of his belief in freedom, in particular. One experimenter believes that psychology, as well as the other behavioral sciences,

> has perhaps done more to solidify, sharpen, and perpetuate,
> thus obfuscate, the division between science and the humani-
> ties than any other "force" in the culture. It has sold to man
> an image of life as being nastier and more brutish, if longer,
> than any that Hobbes could have entertained—an image
> which could leave to the humanist only the role of idle *voy-
> eur* peering tenderly into a sewer. (Koch, 1961).

Many others realize that the only cure for alienation lies in
restoring an essential element of man's self-esteem, a belief in
his own freedom. A growing number of behavioral scientists,
philosophers, science writers, and theologians have dedicated
themselves to doing just that; indeed, salvaging human freedom has become a growth industry! As we noted in the first
chapter, the number of books on freedom has increased astro-
nomically, despite the repeated view that the subject is ex-

hausted. Some titles, such as Rollo May's *Love and Will* and Arthur Koestler's *Act of Creation,* have become best sellers. Myriad others fill up dusty shelves of large university libraries.

A few arguments for freedom are patently absurd, anti-intellectual, antiscientific diatribes. Others, particularly those emanating from theology departments, are so rife with reifications and abstractions as to be unintelligible. On the next few pages we will outline four arguments for human freedom, not because they are correct, but because they are the basic arguments from which all others are derived.

The oldest argument for freedom we will call the *Great Paradox.* It states simply that the "free will–determinism problem has the quality of a paradox because it opposes a poignant universal human experience (freedom of choice) to a most impelling assumption (that there is a reason for everything)" (Barron, 1968). Instead of attempting to resolve the apparent contradiction in favor of one side or the other, we are encouraged to accept the paradox. The origins of this position date back to British philosopher David Hume, although it was William James, the articulate maverick of early American psychology, who first developed the idea. The most vociferous modern advocate of the Great Paradox argument is clinician Carl Rogers (quoted in May, 1967):

> It is my conviction that a part of modern living is to face the paradox that, viewed from one perspective, man is a complex machine. . . . On the other hand, in another dimension of his existence, man is subjectively free; his personal choice and responsibility account for his own life; he is in fact the architect of himself. . . . If in response to this you say, "But these views cannot both be true," my answer is, "This is a deep paradox with which we must learn to live."

If the Great Paradox is the oldest argument for freedom,[14] then the *subject-object* position is the most popular. This second argument was also developed by William James (a prolific man), who distinguished two ways of knowing a

person. There is what he called "the empirical self" (the *me*)
—man treated as a mere object of inquiry that is both predictable and knowable—and there is the "knowing self" (the *I*)—
man experiencing his own life and feeling himself to be a free
agent.

Psychotherapist Rollo May is the most recent popular
advocate of the subject-object distinction. In *Psychology and
the Human Dilemma* (1967), he cites his own behavior as an
example:

> I sit here at my typewriter of a morning writing on one of the
> chapters which follow in this book. As I work, I experience
> myself as a man who has to get a chapter done. . . . I am
> viewing and treating myself as an object, a man to be con-
> trolled and directed in order to perform most effectively the
> task at hand. . . . I treat myself as one who must "fit in"; I
> am gratified at that moment that I am a creature of habit
> without much leeway in behavior; and my aim is to make this
> leeway even less, to control my behavior more rigidly so that
> my chapter will be finished most expeditiously. . . .
>
> But as I continue writing I find myself suddenly caught
> up in an interesting idea. Ah, there is something that has
> been playing around the fringes of my consciousness for years
> —what an alluring prospect to work it out now, form it, see
> where it leads! . . . In this second state—the description of
> which undoubtedly reveals my own bias—I am viewing my-
> self not as object but as subject. My sentences now hinge on
> such verbs as *want, wish, feel,* rather than *have* and *must.*

To be free, argues May, means to balance subjective and
objective states. The individual must be spontaneous enough
to be open to new experiences, to be liberated from habit and
social constraint; yet, once inspired, he must muster the discipline and detachment necessary to implement his wish, desire,
or feeling. Freedom "lies not in my capacity to live as 'pure
subject,' but rather in my capacity to experience both modes,
to live in the dialectical relationship."

The third argument for freedom is the *indeterminism* position. It dates back to the early psychology of William McDougall, who "recognized that prediction could never be exact; that organisms, because they demonstrate purposive behavior, would always be somewhat indeterminate. This indeterminism, he equated with freedom" (Boring, 1929). During the forties and fifties, *indeterminism* received a boost from physics. "The 'uncertainty principle,' first formulated by Heisenberg and further elaborated by Niels Bohr, proclaims essentially a limit of accuracy with which the motion (position and momentum) of a microscopic object can be ascertained, primarily because the process of measurement and observation itself is bound to interfere with the observed particle" (Immergluck, 1964). In *The Measure of Man,* Joseph Wood Krutch (1954) makes extensive use of the indeterminacy principle to rebut the increasing popularity of Skinnerian psychologists in the early fifties:

> They [Skinnerian psychologists] refuse to grant to the individual human being that degree of individuality and unpredictability now granted to the atom and they insist on remaining materialists in a world where matter, as an ultimate persisting reality, has ceased to exist.

A biological version of indeterminism is advanced by George Wald, professor of biology at Harvard. For two reasons, he reminds us, no two cells are identical: First, cells are very complex. Second, they undergo dynamic composition owing to the constant inflow and outflow of energy. This disorder, which is random, is the origin of what Wald defines as freedom.

Actually, physicists for many years have recognized indeterminism as a specious argument. The fact that we cannot measure the action of subatomic particles, they point out, does not mean that these particles operate independently of physical laws. As science philosopher Ernst Nagel reminds us, chance on a subatomic level only means that we are unable to predict what will happen. Indeterminism still persists as an argument for freedom only because it is still widely employed by writers with little understanding of physics.

Indeterminism does have a valid, but tangential, application to the problem of freedom and determinism. It tells us that predictions of human behavior, like certain physical predictions, can be negated by the process of measurement itself. "The key point," writes D. M. MacKay, "is that if what a man believes affects correspondingly the state of his organizing system, no complete up-to-date account of that system could be believed by him without being *ipso facto* rendered out of date" (MacKay, 1966).

The fourth and most effective argument, or, more appropriately, nonargument, for freedom is the *semantic* viewpoint, which says, in effect, that freedom and determinism are abstractions, so let's not bother to talk about them. This argument has widespread influence because it appeals to the scientist's "define your terms" instincts. The semantic tack was first popularized by economist Stuart Chase in *The Tyranny of Words* (1938):

> Is man a free agent, or is he foredoomed by a merciless fate to act thus and so all the days of his life? Such terms are without referents as they stand. They are breeders of bad blood and confusion. When a physicist says that an atom is "free," he does not mean in this context that [an atom] . . . is a rugged individualist with a mind of his own prepared to tolerate no nonsense from an interfering government. He means that the motions of atoms are subject to chance. He uses the word "free" in a statistical sense, talking mathematical language. But sociologists and even biologists associate *responsibility* with "free will"; while the philosopher, unless clubbed into insensibility, will drag the idea into a totally different concept, and, if he belongs to the free-will fraternity, will identify $Atom_1$ with $Adam_1$ (A is A) and triumphantly assert that "science proves the universal principle of free will."

Variations on the semantic approach play subtle games with the words *freedom* and *determinism*. Bertrand Russell, for example, defined determinism as meaning merely a relationship between cause and effect. *Causes do not compel effects; they only proceed them.* From this, he concludes that freedom, which he has not defined, and determinism are compatible.

While Russell defined determinism to make it compatible with freedom, Hobbes defined freedom to make it compatible with determinism. To Hobbes, freedom is the absence of external restriction. Man is free to the extent that he is not constrained. This same argument was repeated by Spinoza and modernized by Abraham Maslow.

"Freedom has now become Spinozistic," Maslow (1966) writes, "i.e., the freedom to embrace and to love one's own destiny, which is certainly determined at least in part by the discovery and the understanding of what and who one is, of one's Real Self."

Many of the preceding arguments may seem familiar to the reader. They may also seem persuasive. They *were* persuasive until now. The power of behavior control technology reduces all four defenses of freedom to insignificance. As Skinner observes with unnerving assurance in *Walden Two*, "Perhaps we can never *prove* that man isn't free; it's an assumption. But the increasing success of a science of behavior makes it more and more plausible." *The arguments fail because they do not try to explain free choice within the framework of science; they try to transcend science, to avoid a confrontation with determinism.* The Great Paradox arbitrarily affirms human freedom. The subject-object argument affirms the illusion of freedom. Indeterminism plays games with science, and the semantic approach plays games with words. All suffer the same fate. When determinism is dramatically demonstrated by the push of a button in one of Delgado's electrode implant experiments, all four defenses of freedom disintegrate.

## Mysticism and Existentialism: The Last Stops?

Where does all this leave our alienated subway rider? If he wants to retain a belief in his freedom, he probably adopts one of two near-hysterical reactions. The first is a complete denial of science. Fallico, for example, dismisses science as some hostile Delphic oracle:

> The so-called sciences which have to do with man and his doings in the world are for the most part a hodge-podge of unwarranted assertions, rationalizations, and undigested commonplaces. . . . The men of this century have accepted the oracular accounts of their being which, emanating from these sources, have made of man, in origin and destiny, a more fearful nonentity than he has ever been before (quoted in Kneller, 1958).

The rejection of science comes primarily from the New Left. (It is spreading rapidly, however. G. R. Taylor warns in *The Biological Time Bomb*, "The day may be approaching when the public turns against science.") Marcuse (1964), for example, blames the development of what he calls "one-dimensional thought" on the scientific method. He rejects scientific philosophy, which, he believes, is "out to exorcise such 'myths' or metaphysical 'ghosts' as Mind, Consciousness, Will, Soul, Self, by disolving the intent of these concepts." Theodore Roszak (1969) advocates the outright rejection of science:

> Nothing less is required than the subversion of the scientific world view, with its entrenched commitment to an egocentric and cerebral mode of consciousness. In its place, there must be a new culture in which the nonintellective capacities of the personality—those capacities that take fire from visionary splendor and experience of human communion—become the arbiters of the good, the true and the beautiful.

Ironically, by rejecting scientific knowledge, the New Left is rejecting its best defense against psytocracy. John Froines, one of the Chicago Seven, and a Ph.D. in chemistry, has warned radicals that they must study science in order to use it humanely. David Riesman agrees. In a recently published conversation, he states:

> The best defense against this [fear of science and scientific manipulation] that I can see is to democratize such manipulative use through education. I believe that social science can be not only useful but also enriching when it meets halfway our curiosity about who we are, and through better knowledge about ourselves, raises our sights as to what we might become.

The second defensive reaction to scientific determinism is existentialism. As Seidel (1966) notes, existentialism "arose in direct opposition to a society, civilization, and view of human life mechanically conceived. Existentialism insisted upon the importance of the individual man and upon individual man's responsibility for what he does or fails to do." In his monumental study of uncommitted students, Kenneth Keniston (1960) notes the extentialist strain of thought among alienated students:

> As of the time when they wrote their philosophies, only one or two of the alienated students had ever read any existentialist works, and none of these had any more than a passing knowledge of existential thought. Yet these young men were for the most part inconscient existentialists, and when, later in their college careers, they were to come upon writers like Sartre, they would sometimes seize on existentialist thought with a sense of *déjà vu.*

Unfortunately, the neo-existentialism of the 1950s backfired, creating further self-degradation and alienation. Despite claims that "*I* is not a fact but an act," existentialism counseled resignation. "Oftentimes this resignation was little more than a grimly stoical acceptance of the absurd," notes Seidel (1966). "It represented defeatism, and in its most extreme forms it advocated, in effect, a philosophy of despair. In many ways existentialism represented a denial of man's basic human power to create." Existentialism proved so depressing in some cases that in 1967 psychiatrist Salvador Maddi identified the emergence of a distinct existential neurosis marked by chronic meaninglessness, apathy, and aimlessness.

It seems that existentialism, like mysticism, is not a very promising way for the individual to challenge scientific determinism and regain his sense of autonomy.

The power of science cannot be denied or rationalized away through the various philosophical tricks we have discussed in this chapter. The ultimate test of science—the prediction and control of human behavior—is met every day with increasing precision in the behavioral science laboratories across the country. If man's sense of freedom is to be restored, it must be expressed within the framework of science. Can this task be accomplished? We have some hope, as we shall demonstrate in the next chapter.

# A FUTURE FOR
# 7   FREEDOM?

*We might paraphrase* The Federalist *papers
by saying, "It seems to have been reserved
to the people of this generation to decide the
important question, whether societies of men
are really capable or not, of establishing
good* teaching *to shape a better society from
reflection and choice, or whether they are
forever destined to depend, for their social
training and social structure on imitation
and accident."*

J. R. Platt
*The Step to Man*

Metaphysical games will not give man the sense of freedom he needs to resist a psytocracy. Although behavior control has grossly oversimplified the image of man, it has firmly
established the lawful nature of human behavior. The question remains whether or not a basis for autonomy can be
found within the framework of behavioral science.

The past decade has witnessed two significant trends in
the science of man. The first, behavior control, we have already explored in some detail. The second trend is the reluctant recognition of human complexity and of the need to return to a study of mental processes. *Reluctant,* because
behavioral scientists would feel more secure with a simple
model of human behavior. Nevertheless, developments inside
and outside the behavioral sciences militate for a long overdue
examination of the human mind. The implications of this

trend for the concept of freedom in particular, and for the future of democracy in general, are profound.

We begin this final chapter, then, with a brief outline of the social and scientific circumstances that are compelling behavioral scientists to recognize the importance of studying complex cognitive human functioning. From there, we move to the emerging science of *process psychology* and to a discussion of possibilities for freedom within the confines of this new perspective on behavior.

## A Contribution from the Cold War

Behavioral scientists owe a debt, of sorts, to the cold war for reminding them of human complexity and the need for studying mental processes. The tensions of international hostilities have required man to act in ways that transcend the capabilities of a simple stimulus-response machine, and the scientist has been forced to take notice of these actions. Although the social system is alienating, it has at least shown that nonmentalistic accounts of human actions are inadequate.

Consider the following question: Will American military assistance to Country X provoke war with the Soviet Union? As one social scientist has pointed out, this is a very simple question requiring, in theory, "some very simple information source, such as a microphone buried in Brezhnev's pschoanalyst's couch." Unfortunately, no such information source exists. Instead, the United States Government commits billions of dollars and man-hours to collecting information on everything from Soviet troop movements to the movements of Brezhnev's family.

Because a simple yes-or-no answer to our question is impossible, we must substitute an enormous quantity of tangential information, which is, in turn, carefully evaluated by groups of political analysts. The evaluation is far from simple. Fact is weighed against fact according to war theory X.

Theory X, in turn, must be measured against theories Y and Z. In addition, analysts must be open to new facts and new theories; the gravity of their job requires a continuous effort to reduce error, which means incorporating as much information as possible into the decision-making process.

Clearly, the analyst who sits at the councils of the RAND Corporation or in the intelligence center of the Pentagon is more than a simple reflex machine. He is constantly sifting vast sums of information, making complex value judgments, and generating new conclusions about the intentions of the Soviet leadership. It would be impossible for us to describe the analyst's behavior in a meaningful way, without taking notice of his mental processes, without learning how his mind operates. To what theory or theories about war does he subscribe? What kinds of facts does he consider important? How does he weigh ideas? Is he receptive to new information? Can he blend a multitude of facts at once? In short, *how does he think?*

The rapid technological changes that characterize cold war society demand that people think more than ever before. Because of the restrictions imposed by organizational democracy, some people may not like what they have to think about; nevertheless, the society places a premium on thought (recall that IBM's motto is "THINK"). Furthermore, the quality of thought demanded has changed. Since ideas are outmoded almost as soon as they are produced, *how* a person thinks becomes more important than what he knows. The original thinker goes for a higher price than the memorizer. In the words of Princeton psychologist Harold Schroder (1971): "In a world characterized by accelerated change . . . what is known becomes less important than process skills: the ability to discover, to generate new information, to seek new relationships and remain flexible and adaptive in the face of environmental fluctuation. . . . In our contemporary world, then, it is not knowing but discovering and conceptualizing that becomes important." The behavioral scientist who deals with practical social problems cannot ignore this fact; he must recognize the complexity and richness of the mind.

## Other Contributions

The cold war has not been the only event to attract the attention of behavioral science to human cognition. The need to understand mental processes has also been underscored by a crisis in contemporary education. Faced with the problem of preparing today's students for tomorrow's challenges with yesterday's pedagogy, teachers and researchers alike are seeking information about how children think so they might devise new methods capable of preparing students for the rigors of the tumultuous times. Educational psychologists are finding out that a simple view of the child's mind leads to a "rote memory" teaching philosophy—a highly dysfunctional procedure in our kaleidoscopic age.

Psychopathology is another area where behavioral scientists are compelled to consider the importance of human mental processes. The pressures of organizational democracy have produced certain "alienation" neuroses that require therapists to obtain extensive knowledge of the patient's thought processes. The existential neurosis, which we mentioned earlier, is one. The famous identity crisis is another. To cure an alienation neurosis (as much as possible within the context of an alienating society), the therapist must come to see the world as his client does. He must understand the mental constructs the client uses to interpret everyday events and then explore the soundness of those constructs with the client. The "cure" in this form of therapy takes place when the client has reformulated his thought processes into a new, more adaptable outlook at the world, or "Gestalt." In other words, the client *adopts a new philosophy of life* (Perls, Hefferline, & Goodman, 1951).

Even behaviorists recognize the importance of dealing with mental processes in therapy. As Dollard and Miller note in *Personality and Psychotherapy* (1950)

> The neurotic is a person who is in need of a stock of sentences that will match the events going on within and without him. The new sentences make possible an immense facilitation of higher mental processes. With their aid he can discriminate and generalize more accurately; he can motivate himself for remote tasks; he can produce hope and caution within himself and aid himself in being logical, reasonable, and planful.

The authors present the example of Mrs. A, who "was very much mixed-up on the matter of eliminative and sexual functions. She had learned as a child that sex was dirty and that defecation was dirty. She tended to react with avoidance to stimuli connected with either drive." In order for Mrs. A to lead a normal sex life, the therapist helped her build a mental sentence to discriminate sex from defecation. "The therapist asserted that these two functions were really very different and tried to help Mrs. A discriminate them sharply."

Ironically, the development of behavior control itself has thrown scientists back to the mind. In the search for a defense against the real and imagined abuses of behavioral science, psychologists have returned to the once forbidden territory of consciousness for what Dr. Anne Roe calls "the forgotten weapon." She writes (1959),

> A potent weapon against [manipulation] . . . is within reach of any who dare to use it. . . . This weapon is, again, self-awareness. The perfect defense against the possibility of manipulation, whether by politicians, priests, or advertisers . . . is to be thoroughly conscious of one's basic needs and attitudes. You cannot be easily manipulated if you know more about yourself than the would-be manipulator does.

## The Return of the Mind

Pressures of the cold war, new demands in education and in mental health, and the reaction to behavior control technology—all are powerful factors militating for a change in the traditionally simplistic view of man. However, the most persuasive arguments for a revised view of the human mind come from linguistics, the science of language and thought. Findings from linguistic studies successfully challenge behaviorism's beliefs that (1) a rejection of mental life is the only route to scientific objectivity, and (2) all actions can be predicted without bothering to understand the human mind.

John Watson, the father of behaviorism, rejected the mind because the introspectionist philosophies inherited from the nineteenth century had reduced behavioral science to an absurd word game. *But Watson forgot about his own mind.* He assumed that behaviorism was objective because it ignored the vagaries of mind, but he neglected to consider his own unconscious prejudices. Linguistics has demonstrated the need to study mental processes, if for no other reason than to detect the hidden biases of the scientist himself. The linguistic argument—linguistic relativity—is as follows: there is no such animal as an objective man. Not even the scientist animal is objective. His thought is determined by the very structure of the language he uses. Therefore, to reject the study of mental processes does not afford objectivity, only the illusion of objectivity. Be failing to account for mental life, the scientist fails to correct the biases imposed by the language he himself uses.

Linguistic relativity is both simple to understand and difficult to recognize. It is simple to understand once we appreciate how much "objective" thought varies from one language to another. However, it is difficult to recognize for the person who is raised within the confines of one language and one culture. It is even more difficult for the traditional scientist to recognize when he assumes that, because he uses scientific jargon, his thoughts are freed from cultural biases. In fact, it is interesting to notice that the man who developed the principle of linguistic relativity never received an advanced degree in any science. Benjamin Lee Whorf, now regarded as one of history's great social scientists, was a successful businessman who studied linguistics only as a hobby. A graduate of M.I.T. with a Bachelor's degree in engineering, he went to work for a fire prevention company, spending his spare time studying the languages of many cultures. From his study Whorf made the revolutionary discovery that:

> The background linguistic system (in other words, the grammar) of each language is not merely a reproducing instrument for voicing ideas but rather is itself the shaper of ideas, the program and guide for the individual's mental activity, for his analysis of impressions, for his synthesis of his mental stock in trade. Formulation of ideas is not an independent process, strictly rational in the old sense, but is part of a particular grammar, and differs, from slightly to greatly, between different grammars. (Whorf, 1956).

Whorf writes that no individual is capable of describing nature with absolute impartiality; he is always restricted to certain thought patterns, even when he thinks he is most free. Anyone who talks about objectivity, Whorf asserts, "is apt to be simply marching in step with purely grammatical facts that have somewhat of a background character in his own language or family of languages but are by no means universal in all languages and in no sense a common substratum of reason."

The so-called objectivity of behaviorism, Whorf concludes, is a deception; the behaviorist is still influenced by unconscious linguistic prejudices, perhaps even more than the nonbehaviorist who is less cocksure of his preconceptions. He reminds psychologists that they cannot hope to develop an accurate picture of human behavior without taking into account the mental filters that color their perceptions of it.

The work of Whorf, taken alone, is enough to shake the

credibility of behaviorism but not to bring it tumbling down. He shows us that the mind cannot be excluded from psychology—that Watson was wrong to assume that a blanket rejection of mental life is the proper route to scientific objectivity. Yet Whorf's findings do not severely challenge Watson's second supposition that all actions can be predicted without bothering to understand the mind. This leads us to the second critical impact of linguistics: the demonstration that an adequate explanation of some human actions (specifically verbal behavior) is impossible without taking into account internal psychological processes.

Karl Lashley (1951) was one of the first scientists to challenge behavioristic thought with an examination of human verbal communication. Behaviorists had regarded words as specific auditory stimuli, each of which elicited exact verbal or behavioral responses from the listener. Such a simple stimulus-response view of communication encouraged the scientist to ignore the human mind when investigating verbal behavior. Lashley showed the fallacy in the behaviorist viewpoint. Like Whorf's argument for linguistic relativity, his reasoning was simple. (So simple, it had eluded experimental psychologists for over 40 years.) It is impossible for people to understand each other, Lashley demonstrated, without thought mechanisms to filter words and to interrelate word meanings. Words are not received by the mind as separate stimuli. On the contrary,

> Words stand in relation to the sentence as letters do to the words: the words themselves have no intrinsic temporal "valence." The word *right,* for example, is a noun, adjective, adverb, and verb, and has four spellings and at least ten meanings. In such a sentence "the millwright on my right thinks it right that some conventional rite should symbolize the right of every man to write as he pleases," word arrangement is obviously not due to any direct association of the word *right* itself with other words, but to the meanings which are determined by some broader relations.

Since Lashley, linguists have produced several instances of verbal behavior that are impossible to explain within the antimentalistic framework of behaviorism. Three-year-old children, for example, are able to speak original sentences without ever hearing them before and without coaxing from parents or other authority figures. Such a feat is only possible if the child has developed the mental capacity to piece together complex ideas and to translate these ideas into formal grammar. M.I.T. psycholinguist Noam Chomsky, the acknowledged leader of the linguistic revolt against traditional behavioral theories, has outlined a psychology of *transformational grammar*. In brief, Chomsky argues that thought is far more than a simple chain-reaction reflex; it is a building process. The mind is a complex of rules for translating, evaluating, and generating language. The uttered sentence is, therefore, not merely a verbal reflex; it is the product of extensive mental manipulation.

To summarize, linguistics has forced psychology back to a study of mental processes in two ways. First, it has shown that behaviorism contradicts itself by ignoring the mentality of behaviorists; or, in the words of science philosopher A. O. Lovejoy (1922), "Behaviorism belongs to that class of theories which becomes absurd as it becomes articulate." Second, linguistics has demonstrated that behavior cannot be adequately explained without reference to mental processes. Summarizing the impact of linguistics on the problem of mind, Chomsky (1968) writes:

> If we accept a realistic statement of the problem, I believe we will also be forced to accept a more cognitive approach to it; to talk about hypothesis testing instead of discrimination learning, to talk about the evaluation of hypotheses instead of the reinforcement of responses, about rules instead of habits, about productivity instead of generalization, about innate and universal human capacities instead of special methods of teaching vocal responses, about symbols instead of conditioned stimuli, about sentences instead of words or vocal noises, about linguistic structure instead of chains of responses —in short, about language instead of learning theory.

## The Rise of Process Psychology

In response to renewed interest in studying the mind, a new psychology is emerging. It is not yet a school, so it does not have a name. For our purposes, we will call it *process psychology*. Its advocates come from a wide range of disciplines: psychology, anthropology, communications, and sociology. However, the apostles of process psychology have one interesting trait in common: most, if not all, are, or have been, deeply involved with practical social problems. M.I.T.'s Noam Chomsky is a well-known political activist. Harvard psychologist Jerome Bruner has written extensively on educational problems. George Kelly, Harold Schroder, Frederick Perls, and Paul Goodman have backgrounds in clinical psychology. The European sociologist, Jacques Ellul, was heavily involved in French politics.

Process psychology takes the following stances about mental behavior:

First, it rejects behaviorism. Process psychology recognizes that *the brain (or nervous system) is a highly elaborate information-processing organ.* It has the ability to develop, work, and rework ideas or concepts in myriad ways. In a prophetic journal article on purposive behavior in animals and men, psychologist Edward Tolman (1948) anticipates this view of the brain:

[The brain] is far more like a map control room than it is like an old fashioned telephone exchange. The stimuli, which are allowed in, are not connected by just simple one-to-one switches to the outgoing responses. Rather, the incoming impulses are usually worked over and elaborated in the central control room into a tentative, cognitive-like map of the environment. And it is this tentative map, indicating routes and paths and environmental relationships, which finally determines what responses, if any, the animal will finally release.

Man, being the most sophisticated animal, has a very extensive internal mapping network. He has over 10 billion neurons, or brain cells. Although each cell has only two possibilities, to fire or not to fire, the possible variations in thought patterns and ideas are almost infinite.

Second, *the quality of thought, or information processing, varies among people.* Some people make very simplistic judgments based on little information and few criteria; others make far more complex judgments, using as much information as possible to generate as many alternative ideas as possible. Bruner, for example, has discovered that to solve the same problem different people employ different cognitive strategies, some more complex than others. Schroder has found much the same thing. He identifies the complexity of a person's thinking in terms of how "concrete" or "abstract" it is. "Concretes" are intolerant of ambiguity, dogmatic, rigid, and closed-minded. They are also overly dependent on external authority for their ideas, ideals, and ideology. "Abstract" persons, on the other hand, are independent, tolerant of ambiguity, and adaptable to change.

The quality of thought has little to do with *what* a person knows, but rather *how he uses* what he knows. That a person has amassed a great quantity of factual information is no guarantee that he can use this information creatively to develop new ideas. We all have met at least one human computer during our high school or college days. He was the kid who memorized the math textbook verbatim. He knew exactly where the commas came in the geometry postulates. But give him an original problem and his immediate response is: INSUFFICIENT DATA. Process psychology equates quality with sophistication, not storage capacity: it wants to know how a person uses his mind. Consider the following experiment, a game: The subject is presented with a problem. Two hypothetical countries, Slabovia and Ubanga, are at war. The subject is given access to all the information he needs to know about these countries, such as population count, geography, armaments, alliances, and so on. The subject's task is to negotiate a peace agreement between the two countries. In such an experiment, there is no one right answer. Several possible solutions exist. The experimenters are interested in measuring how the subject's mind deals with the problem. What kind of information does he seek about Slabovia and Ubanga? How broad is his information search? How unique is his solution? How many tentative solutions does he devise? The goal of this experiment is not to measure how much information the subject can store, but how he *uses* the information that is available. In its emphasis on the style of thought, processing psychology echoes the early writings of Erich Fromm (1941):

> The pathetic superstition prevails that by knowing more and more facts one arrives at knowledge of reality. Hundreds of scattered and unrelated facts are dumped into the heads of students; their time and energy are taken up by learning more and more facts so that there is little left for thinking. To be sure, thinking without a knowledge of facts remains empty and fictitious; but "information" alone can be just as much an obstacle to thinking as the lack of it.

Third, *the quality of thought varies, not only among people, but within a single individual.* People devote little thought to subjects that to them are dull and uninteresting; they devote a lot more thought to topics that are personally relevant or enticing. This is almost axiomatic. A lawyer would take a far more sophisticated approach to law than to art history. The reverse would be true for an art historian.

Fourth, *the quality of thought is not directly related to intelligence as measured by so-called IQ tests.* The quality of information processing (thinking), according to Schroder (1967), does not parallel performance on standard recall and IQ tests, but is highly correlated with performance on essay and originality tests. In this sense, when process psychologists talk about complex thinkers they are speaking about individuals that most people would call "creative" (Karlins, 1967,

1968). It is these complex thinkers who can utilize information in new and meaningful ways in solving problems, who have the capacity to remain flexible and adaptive in the face of change and uncertainty.

This brings us to process psychology's final—and most important—statement about human behavior: *the quality of thought is not a given; it is the product of training and experience.* Simple thought patterns are not born; they are made. They are the outcome of simplistic environments at home and at school, where parents and teachers provide a child with ready-made rules and then control his behavior by means of rewards and punishments until he learns to follow them. The relationship between the authority figure and the child is "analogous to that of a doctor and his patient or a programmer and a computer. The child, like the patient or the computer, is a passive recipient of information transmitted by the training agent: that is, it is 'fed into him' and acted upon in a spirit of rote compliance" (Schroder, Karlins & Phares, 1971). Such training creates an individual who adapts by looking to authority figures for guidance. Traditionally, most methods of teaching in education and industry have relied on these authoritarian training methods. Similarly, most parents rely heavily on such methods, telling a child what is good and bad, rewarding or punishing him accordingly.

Complex thinking is the result of experience that teaches the individual, not to follow rules blindly, but to think for himself. More correctly, he is taught the supreme rule: question everything. (If we want to look "into truth," wrote Descartes, "it is necessary once in one's life to doubt of all things, so far as this is possible.") In terms of education, training complex thinkers involves letting the student learn by receiving feedback as a consequence of his own questions or exploratory behavior. The teacher does not supply the learner with a neat package marked "Ready-Made Rules for Thinking and Interpreting Your Existence." Instead, the teacher (or parent) encourages the child to develop his own perspectives, theories, and ideas about the world, without relying on external authority. In such an educational environment,

> the child is judged not by the amount of information he has accumulated and can recall but by how effectively he can utilize information at his disposal in coping with his environment; not by what he has memorized but the process by which he attained the information he memorized. The training agent in process education acts more as a guide than an authority directing the child: he is there to help the youngster solve his problems, not to tell him how they are to be solved (Schroder, Karlins & Phares, 1971).

It is important to note that the training conditions that produce complex thinking are just as controlled, if not more so, than the conditions that produce simpler modes of information processing. It is easier to dictate to a child than it is to construct a situation that teaches him to teach (and think for) himself.

## Freedom Revisited

What are the implications of this new psychology for man's concept of freedom? If we ask ourselves what we mean by complex thought processes—generating new ideas, evaluating information in different ways, choosing among alternatives —are we not really talking about freedom? Man has the mental potential to modify his knowledge constantly; this potential for learning is the potential for freedom. Schroder defines freedom as "the ability of a person to produce his own conceptions, to generate alternative and conflicting conceptions, to think and value in terms of multiple perspectives, and to define one's identity and his relationships to others on the basis of these self-generated conceptions of the world" (Schroder, Karlins & Phares, 1971). Similarly, Frank Barron (1968) writes, "The essence of our human freedom . . . is this, that matter has acquired the capacity to work radical modifications in itself. Thus, among its 'available responses' is the ability to act in such a manner as to increase its own flexibility, or deliberately to maximize its own response variability."

Since processing skills vary from simple to complex, and since these skills, in turn, are related to training, freedom is not the opposite of scientific determinism. Freedom is a *quality of determinism*. When conflict arises, the man with simple information-processing skills will fall back on ethical systems, serial sets of priorities, and other external criteria. His behavior is determined in the rigid, classical sense of the word. The free man, on the other hand, *has been determined* to resolve his conflicts by generating new ideas and concepts.

Some people will object to this notion of freedom. This is understandable. They are infected by the long-standing distinction between scientific determinism and freedom, which we discussed in the last chapter. But let us stop and think what is really meant by freedom. As psychobiologist Roger Sperry (1965) pointed out in a lecture on brain research and humanism, the ideal free-will machine would not be free from environmental determinism; on the contrary, like the complex information processor, he would be most attuned to environment:

> I suspect . . . that if you were assigned the task of trying to design and build the perfect free will model . . . you might decide that your aim should not be so much to free the machinery from causal contact as the opposite; that is, to try to incorporate into your model the potential value of universal causal contact—in other words, contact with all related information in proper proportion, past, present, and future.

Sperry notes that freedom, in any meaningful sense, is determinism from within:

> To a very real and large extent, a person does determine with his own mind what he is going to do from a large number of

possibilities. This does not mean, however, that he is free from the forces of his own decision making machinery. [He is determined] by the combined effects of his own thoughts, his own reasoning, his own feeling, his own beliefs, ideals, and hopes.

Once we understand that freedom is a high level of information processing, then other writings on freedom begin to make more sense. For example, Julian Huxley argued in 1957 that freedom required a new synthesis of ideas: "One of the intellectual urgencies of today is to reorganize thought, wherever it is still dualistic, under the head of new unitary concepts." A decade later, Marcuse argued the opposite: that freedom requires the rejection of unitary concepts, what he calls "one-dimensional thought." Both men were half right; freedom is not defined by ideas but by action. It is a continuous integrative process of synthesis, division, and synthesis.[15] As Jacques Ellul cogently observes in his introduction to *The Technological Society* (1964), freedom requires continuous conflict within the individual. If prevailing ideas are fragmented, the free man must bring them together; if a single idea dominates, he must attack it. Scientific skepticism in all spheres of life would be the epitome of freedom—it would call for open-ended information processing and for tentative solutions to all problems.

Process psychology preserves the idea of freedom, but not without some revolutionary modifications. Traditionally, we have thought of freedom as a "given" quality, something man has at birth, like a soul. Debates on the free will–determinism issue hinged on the question, "Does man have free will?" meaning does he possess the quality of freedom? Process psychology does not treat freedom as a "given" ability, but as a skill, which may or may not develop, depending on the social conditions in which an individual is raised. Furthermore, the new psychology slights our egalitarian sensibilities by suggesting that freedom is a variable, that one person can be more or less free than another.

Another dramatic change in the concept of freedom is

the role of conflict and struggle. Freedom is not, as the poet Robert Frost once said, "moving easy in harness." It is dynamic, writes Ellul (1964), "not a vested interest, but a prize continually to be won. The moment man stops and resigns himself, he becomes subject to determinism. He is most enslaved when he thinks he is comfortably settled in freedom."

## Programming People for Freedom

Perhaps the most revolutionary aspect of the new freedom is its dependence on carefully controlled conditioning techniques for implementation in the individual. It is also the hardest proposition for us to accept on a "gut" emotional level. All the science fiction we have read for the past half-century has warned that behavior control implies tyranny. To accept the fact that all behavior is controlled is difficult enough, even for a scientist. But to equate freedom with control! Nevertheless, complex thinking processes are the result of very sophisticated childhood training environments. Teaching a child to be an automaton is easy. Just instruct him in a few pat rules of behavior and reward him with praise or a candy bar for being "a good boy." He will be very happy, very well behaved (predictable), and very unfree. Teaching a child freedom, however, involves a far more intricate system of behavior control. The free child is encouraged to initiate his own behavior, to devise his own questions and the means for answering them. His training environment, therefore, must be programmed to meet any possible interest the child might develop. And since the child is encouraged to generate his own answers to problems, the parent or teacher must be able to discern and reward originality, without encouraging haphazard guesswork or random idiocy at the same time.

Finally, teaching freedom requires control because it is a delicate process. Just as simple conditions will produce simple thought processes, so will overly complex ones.

In the most general sense [writes Schroder (1967)], conditions that are either oversimple or overcomplex lead to the arrest of development at some point along the concrete-abstract dimension. Conditions that produce too much diversity will eventually retard development of effective schemata for integration, and result in more concrete structure. Conversely, conditions that fail to produce enough diversity, conflict, or complexity, retard the development of abstract system properties.

In simple language Schroder tells us that optimum mental development requires a balanced conditioning environment. The inquiring child should be free to explore his world, but we must make sure that he and his world are ready for each other. If the child is not challenged enough, he will stagnate. However, if the child is challenged too much, if he is overwhelmed, he will also stagnate. Preparing a child to be a thoughtful, and therefore free, adult means that his mind must be carefully nurtured at its maximum potential.

Freedom through open but controlled environments is the basis of progressive education as originally conceived by John Dewey and Mme. Maria Montessori. Unfortunately, the foundations of progressive education have been grossly misinterpreted by modern educators. Freedom has been equated with license, and the importance of a programmed environment has been forgotten. The result is the failure of so-called progressive education and the reactionary call for the "good old" authoritarian methods. What must be understood is that authoritarian and permissive techniques are two sides of the same coin. Both reduce the scope of individual functioning, authoritarianism by emphasizing rote learning and permissiveness by failing to provide learning with form and consistency. Only an education that accommodates student initiative within the framework of a structured environment can cultivate the freedom of higher processing skills.

And what about alienated man's self-concept? Can it be repaired sufficiently to shield him against the lure of a psytocracy? Process psychology does not automatically make man free; it only tells man that he is capable of freedom—with considerable effort on his part. The grown adult does not have the benefit of an education for freedom. His thought processes certainly are less sophisticated than they might be under ideal circumstances. Even the most "open-minded" adult often grounds his thoughts in external authority figures and status hierarchies of which he is not even aware. To make himself free, today's alienated man will have to make a continuous, and seemingly unnatural, effort to try new experiences and to question old ideas. The task of bridging psychological life styles will, of course, be difficult. "Such destruction of the status quo may arouse fear, interruption, and anxiety"; but ultimately "the process is accompanied by the security of the new invention experimentally coming into being" (Perls, Hefferline & Goodman, 1951).

And what about our children? Programming them for freedom will not be easy within the psychological context of organizational democracy. It will call for difficult and dramatic changes in educational institutions. Traditional methods of instruction call for children to develop patterns of dominance and submission, and to look to external sources for guidance. In short, they teach a child to be uncomfortable standing alone. Process methods, which teach self-reliance, augment feelings of self-worth, and make the person more willing to explore his world, are more difficult to accomplish. Things aren't helped by the prevalent hostility of teachers toward free and creative children. As psychologist E. Paul Torrance noted: "Society is downright savage towards creative thinkers, especially when they are young."

The hope for widespread freedom programming lies in the willingness of enlightened parents to learn enough about behavior modification to supervise the education of their children properly. Hope also lies in the technology of automated devices and computers, with their potential for producing complex information-processing learning environments. But we cannot be overly optimistic. Freedom, as Fromm pointed out over 30 years ago, is difficult to achieve. The appeals to regressive authoritarianism are strong. The route to freedom and, therefore, to a genuine participatory democracy for ourselves and our children will be trying. At least we can begin the journey firm in the conviction that freedom can be ours if we are willing to pursue it.

# AFTERTHOUGHT: IS FREEDOM WORTH THE EFFORT?

**8**

> *If we wish to remain human, then there is only one way, the way into the open society. We must go on into the unknown, the uncertain and insecure, using what reason we may have to plan as well as we can for both, security and freedom.*
>
> Karl Popper
> *The Open Society and Its Enemies*

It should be obvious to the reader that throughout this book we have indicated a preference for participatory democracy over psytocracy. We assume that most readers share our judgment. After all, the concept of personal liberty, implicit in democracy, connotes a whole universe of "good" meanings—freedom, justice, independence, Lincoln, the Bill of Rights, and so on—that have been instilled in us since childhood.

Nevertheless, we should ask ourselves, "Why participatory democracy?" If democracy and psytocracy are both the product of conditioning, and if people can "fit into" either social system, why opt for democracy? After all, it is the more difficult social system to build and maintain. The forces in society that push for democracy have already produced a great deal of social and cognitive stress, and we can certainly expect more, at least initially, from any attempt to establish genuine participatory democracies. Furthermore, psytocracy offers security, and we would be hypocrites if we denied the appeal of a stable existence. No less a man than Thomas Henry Huxley once wrote, "If some great power would agree to make me always think what is true and do what is right, on condition of being turned into sort of a clock and being wound up every morning before I got out of bed, I should instantly close with the offer" (quoted in Skinner, 1955–1956).

The authors are reminded of an incident that took place during a seminar on "Utopias and Dystopias" at Princeton University in the fall of 1967. Fourteen participants, including the authors, were discussing the horrors of Aldous Huxley's *Brave New World,* when number 15 stood up and said, "What's wrong with it? After all, the people who lived in the society thought it was all right." No one else agreed with the lone dissenter, but he had a point. If the Alphas and the Betas and the Gammas were happy, what was so wrong with the society?

Various reasons can be given for choosing participatory democracy over psytocracy, but from the authors' viewpoint the best argument was implied by William James over 70 years ago. Our present realm of consciousness, he argued, is but one of many possible states of consciousness. Our perceptions represent but one world, while our minds have the potential to visit many more. This contention is dramatically demonstrated by the linguistic studies of Benjamin Lee Whorf and by the disjointed nature of scientific progress as outlined by Thomas Kuhn in *The Structure of Scientific Revolutions.* Psytocracy perpetuates prevailing ideas; it is a closed loop. Participatory democracy, as a way of life, challenges the mind to new ideas; it is open-ended. While psytocracy offers intellectual security, democracy leaves us open to explore unknown universes.

To paraphrase the ending of a science-fiction novel by Isaac Asimov, the difference between psytocracy and participatory democracy is the difference between what man is and what he can become. Psytocracy guarantees eternity; participatory democracy is the prelude to infinity.

# Notes

1. Today some investigators choose to call these "centers" brain "areas" to emphasize that they are not as circumscribed as once believed.
2. The *New York Times* has not forgotten Delgado. On September 19, 1970 they published a second editorial dealing with his work and its Orwellian implications. The two editorials are strikingly similar in tone and content.
3. There is a problem with Goorney's use of behavior modification. During his nine days of therapy the compulsive gambler suffered recurrent anxiety attacks. At one point, Dr. Goorney states, "The patient expressed the opinion that it was only the realization that he must obtain a cure that was keeping him going." One wonders if less motivated or more anxious individuals would have continued in therapy. It could well be that negative reinforcement is limited in therapeutic usefulness to people who are highly motivated to overcome their problems.
4. The "telescreen" was a formidable behavior control device

used in George Orwell's fiercely regulated society of *1984*. A "two-way" TV set where the viewer became the viewed, the telescreen was used by the government to monitor the behavior of its citizenry. Besides discouraging seditious activity (who would dare rebel under the watchful gaze of the ever-present camera eye?), the telescreen also served as a superb information-gathering device, a chronicler of each citizen's life history.

And the information it garnered didn't go to waste but was imaginatively used by the ruling inner party membership to control the actions of individual citizens. In the case of Orwell's protagonist Winston, for example, telescreen-gathered information about his fear of rats was used to crush his heretical political views and win him over to party doctrine. The philosophy underlying telescreen use is of interest to us here: *The more you know about a person, the better your chances of controlling his behavior.*

5.  See, for example, M. Karlins, *The Last Man Is Out* (Englewood Cliffs, N.J.: Prentice-Hall, 1969), in which behavior modification principles are combined with computer technology to direct the destiny of a major league baseball team.

6.  For the reader who seeks additional information on LSD, an excellent bibliography is provided in Charles Tart's book, *States of Altered Consciousness* (New York: Wiley, 1969), pp. 480–483.

7.  A new emphasis on behavior control research in American universities has also swelled the rolls of scientists working on the manipulation of human actions. Gardner Quarton explains why:

> Until quite recently the medical doctor was one of the few professionals with both a major interest in modifying human behavior and personality, and a biological interest in the brain. His concern arose directly from his therapeutic activities. He knew, understood, and presumably liked his neighbors and patients. He was, however, usually so busy with the demands of practice and so compelled to act with inadequate knowledge that he seldom reflected on alternate explanations of behavior and rarely conducted systematic experiments. As a result, sci-

entific knowledge of the determinants of human behavior has developed very slowly. With the development of modern academic medicine, the concept has spread that doctors can be investigative human biologists. In the last few years this idea has been extended to psychiatry, neurology, and neurosurgery. This had led to a rapid increase in research effort and has supplied a group of highly skilled technicians who have extended the findings of animal biology and psychology by human experiments. During the same period, with the development of molecular genetics, biology—as it is taught in the universities—has become less naturalistic and more experimental. Not only are careers in experimental biology possible outside medicine, but much of the really significant progress has occurred there. Psychology as a laboratory science has developed apace. Many dedicated, full-time investigators are working intensively on the determinants of human behavior. It seems very likely, then, that we can expect a rapid increase in the scientific knowledge about the way in which the brain works and the way in which environmental factors interact with biological events to produce complex behavior (Quarton, 1967).

8.  Contrary to the suppositions of most fiction writers, these procedures are not the most effective behavior control measures. Consider brainwashing. In reality, it is neither very new nor very effective. This was pointed out by Edgar Schein in a now classic study conducted on American servicemen repatriated from North Korean prison camps. In the case of the so-called truth serums (commonly sodium amytal or sodium pentothal), Lawrence Freedman made the following observation in a *Scientific American* article back in 1960:

> Experimental and clinical findings indicate that only individuals who have conscious and unconscious reasons for doing so are inclined to confess and yield to interrogation under the influence of drugs. On the other hand, some people are able to withhold information and some, especially character neurotics, are able to lie. Others are

> so suggestible or so impelled by unconscious guilt that they will describe, perhaps in response to suggestive questioning, behavior that never in fact occurred.

As is clear from Freedman's commentary, the person who depends on "truth drugs" to control another's behavior is putting his faith in a very unreliable and resistible form of persuasion.

In the study of hypnosis no sizable amount of scientific evidence has ever been accumulated to indicate that a person in a hypnotic trance can be made to do something he would not voluntarily do in a waking state. A common story relevant to this point concerns a hypnotist who induced a female subject, under hypnosis, to perform many types of behavior at his command. Yet when he asked the girl to remove her blouse, she snapped out of her trance and sent the startled hypnotist reeling with a resounding slap across the face! In his book *Techniques of Persuasion,* Dr. J. Brown (1963) puts it this way: "The committing of socially reprehensible acts under hypnosis cannot be excluded as a possibility, but it is of far too rare and unreliable a nature to be counted on by those with evil intentions."

9. We must differentiate here between synthetic and actual experience. We are constantly reminded how the mass media have expanded human awareness. But we must remember that television, radio, films, and newspapers are vicarious experiences that enrich the intellect, but not the physical self.

10. We recommend Huxley's *Brave New World* and Fromm's *Revolution of Hope* for more detailed descriptions of psytocracy and participatory democracy, respectively. For a more thorough analysis of our present organizational democracy, works by Riesman, Roszak, and Galbraith (see bibliography) are excellent sources.

11. A new book has just been published that is relevant to this idea. See A. Toffler, *Future Shock* (New York: Random House, 1970).

12. The pre-Christian Western philosophers, who took a far broader perspective on human behavior than their modern counterparts, did not make arbitrary distinctions between body and soul. The ancients sought a unified science of man; their

goal was to explain, not only simple human and animal actions, such as reflexes, but also the more complex psychological activities such as thinking, imagination, and choice. Although the theories they produced were hardly sound from the viewpoint of the modern scholar, their goal of a comprehensive science of man was noble. Furthermore, they managed to generate some ideas that only recently have been recognized as having insight. Epicurus (342?–270 B.C.), for example, defined the soul as "the most subtle form of that substance" that comprises the universe. His theory that free will exists in the random fluctuation of soul atoms was a prophesy of the "uncertainty principle" in modern physics (Hall, 1969).

13. Before continuing, we should say something in Watson's defense. Modern critics of behaviorism, particularly Arthur Koestler, have been unfair to Watson, accusing him of every academic sin from naïveté to ignorance. Behaviorism must be understood in the context of the times. By the turn of the century, introspective psychology had generated so much semantic haze that scientists could no longer talk to each other. German psychologist Wilhelm Wundt, who had proposed that psychology be limited to the analysis of consciousness by trained introspectionists, precipitated a plethora of contradictory studies. For example, Külpe in Germany "proved" the existence of irreconcilable thought with his trained introspectionists, while Titchener in America with his trained introspectionists "disproved" imageless thought. Mentalistic arguments had developed to such absurd proportions that psychologists grew "restive under conventional restraints. They were finding the old problems lifeless and thin, they were 'half sick of shadows,' and, turning gladly toward something that seemed more alive and substantial, they welcomed a plain, downright revolt" (Heibdreder, 1939). In Watson's time, behaviorism was a logical and even beneficial step for psychology. It helped to clarify points and to put the science of behavior into a manageable perspective.

Behaviorism became a problem only when it stopped being a science and became a religion. The purpose of any scientific theory is to serve as a tool for uncovering knowledge; a good scientist never accepts a theory as literal truth. Unfortunately, after theories become established, they frequently become dogma. This is what happened to behaviorism. In 1939 historian of psychology Edna Heidbreder observed that "behaviorism has become more than a mere school of psychology; it has become a crusade against the enemies of science, and in this role it has taken on, even more than have most schools of psychology, something of the character of a cult." She summarizes the attitudes of behaviorists this way: "On the right hand side are behaviorism and science and all its works; on the left are souls and superstition and a mistaken tradition."

14. We acknowledge that there is not complete agreement on this point. Some historians find traces of the subject-object distinction in the writings of Aristotle.

15. The neurotic is the person who has lost this integrative ability to the point where he can no longer function adequately. The goal of therapy is to restructure the neurotic thought processes, making them flexible enough so that the person can cope realistically with the environment (Perls, Hefferline, & Goodman, 1951).

# References

Allen, S. Sad story of stocks. *San Francisco Chronicle,* June 16, 1970, 50.

Amis, K. *New maps of hell.* New York: Harcourt, 1960.

Argyris, C. *Integrating the individual and the organization.* New York: Wiley, 1964.

Asimov, I. *End of eternity.* New York: Lancer, 1956.

Atwood, K. Discussion—part one. In T. M. Sonneborn (Ed.), *The control of human heredity and evolution.* New York: Macmillan, 1965. Pp. 35–38.

Augustinus. The free choice of the will. In R. P. Russell, O.S.A. (Trans.), *The fathers of the church,* Vol. 59. Washington, D.C.: Catholic University of America Press, 1968. Pp. 62–243.

Augustinus. Free will and God's foreknowledge. In N. E. Cantor and P. L. Klein (Eds.), *Augustine and Thomas Aquinas.* Waltham, Mass.: Blaisdell, 1969.

Axline, V. *Dibs: In search of self.* Boston: Houghton Mifflin, 1964.

Barron, F. The psychology of creativity. In *New directions in psychology II*. New York: Holt, Rinehart and Winston, 1965. Pp. 1–134.

Barron, F. *Creativity and personal freedom*. Princeton, N. J.: Van Nostrand, 1968.

Bauer, R. *The new man in soviet psychology*. Cambridge, Mass.: Harvard University Press, 1952.

Becker, E. *The structure of evil*. New York: Braziller, 1968.

Bennis, W. Post-bureaucratic leadership. *Transaction*, 1969, **6**, July/August, 44–52.

Bennis, W., & Harris, T. G. Warren Bennis, a conversation. *Psychology Today*, 1970, **3**, February, 48–54, 68–71.

Bernard, C. *An introduction to the study of experimental medicine*. New York: Dover, 1957.

Bettelheim, B. Joey: A "mechanical boy." *Scientific American*, 1959, **200**, March, 116–127.

Blackburn, P. Meditation on the BMT. In P. Leary and R. Kelly (Eds.), *A controversy of poets*. New York: Doubleday, 1965.

Blauner, R. Work satisfaction and industrial trends in modern society. In W. Galenson and S. Lipset (Eds.), *Labor and trade unionism: An interdisciplinary reader*. New York: Wiley, 1960. Pp. 339–360.

Boring, E. G. *A history of experimental psychology*. New York: Appleton-Century-Crofts, 1929.

Branden, N. *The psychology of self-esteem*. Los Angeles: Nash Publishing Company, 1969.

Brett, G. *A history of psychology, I*. New York: Macmillan, 1921.

Brett, G. *Psychology ancient and modern*. New York: Longmans, 1928.

Bridgeman, P. Quo Vadis. In P. Obler and H. Estrin (Eds.), *The new scientist*. New York: Anchor, 1962. Pp. 302–312.

Brown, J. A. *Techniques of persuasion*. Baltimore: Penguin, 1963.

Brown, R. *Social psychology*. New York: Free Press, 1965.

Bruner, J. *Towards a theory of instruction*. Cambridge, Mass.: Harvard University Press, 1966.

Bruner, J., Goodnow, J., & Austin, G. *A study in thinking*. New York: Wiley, 1956.

Budrys, A. Mind control is good—bad (check one). *Esquire*, 1966, May, 106–109.

Burrows, D., & Lapides, F. (Eds.), *Alienation: A casebook*. New York: Crowell, 1969.

Chase, S. *The tyranny of words*. New York: Harcourt, 1938.

Chomsky, N. *Language and mind*. New York: Harcourt, 1968.

Clarke, A. *Profiles of the future*. New York: Harper & Row, 1963.

Compton, D. *Synthajoy*. New York: Ace Books, 1968.

Davis, K. Sociological aspects of genetic control. In J. Roslansky (Ed.), *Genetics and the future of man*. New York: Appleton-Century-Crofts, 1966. Pp. 173–204.

Davison, G. Elimination of a sadistic fantasy by a client-controlled counter-conditioning technique. *Journal of Abnormal Psychology*, 1968, **73**, 84–90.

Delgado, J. *Physical control of the mind*. New York: Harper & Row, 1969.

Dewey, J. *Freedom and culture*. New York: Putnam, 1939.

Diggory, J. *Self-evaluation: Concepts and studies*. New York: Wiley, 1966.

Dollard, J., & Miller, N. *Personality and psychotherapy*. New York: McGraw-Hill, 1950.

Dostoevsky, F. *The grand inquisitor*. New York: Ungar, 1956.

Eliot, T. S. "The hollow men." In *Collected poems*. New York: Harcourt, 1934.

Ellul, J. *The technological society*. New York: Knopf, 1964.

Feigl, H. The philosophical embarrassments of psychology. *American Psychologist*, 1959, **14**, 125–126.

Field, E. Unwanted. *Stand up, friend, with me*. New York: Grove, 1963.

Freedman, L. "Truth" drugs. *Scientific American*, 1960, **202**, 145–154.

Fromm, E. *Escape from freedom*. New York: Holt, Rinehart and Winston, 1941.

Fromm, E. *The sane society*. New York: Holt, Rinehart and Winston, 1955.

Fromm, E. *The revolution of hope*. New York: Harper & Row, 1968.

Fuller, P. Operant conditioning of a vegetative human organism. *American Journal of Psychology*, 1949, **62**, 587–590.

Galbraith, J. *The new industrial state*. Boston: Houghton Mifflin, 1967.

Goodman, P. *Growing up absurd.* New York: Random House, 1956.

Goorney, A. Treatment of a compulsive horse race gambler by aversion therapy. *British Journal of Psychiatry,* 1968, 114, 329–333.

Grunbaum, A. Causality and the science of human behavior. *American Scientist,* 1952, 40, 665–676.

Hall, T. *Ideas of life and matter.* Chicago: University of Chicago Press, 1969.

Hamblin, R., Buckholdt, D., Bushell, D., Ellis, D., & Ferritor, D. Changing the game from "get the teacher" to "learn." *Transaction,* 1969, January, 20–31.

Hausknecht, M. The mike in the bosom. *Dissent,* 1957, 4, 56–59.

Heath, R. Electrical self-stimulation of the brain in man. *American Journal of Psychiatry,* 1963, 120, 571–577.

Heidbreder, R. *Seven psychologies.* New York: Appleton-Century-Crofts, 1939.

Himwich, H. The new psychiatric drugs. *Scientific American,* 1955, 193, October, 80–86.

Huxley, A. *Brave new world.* New York: Doubleday, 1932.

Huxley, A. *Island.* New York: Harper & Row, 1962.

Huxley, J. *New bottles for new wine.* New York: Harper & Row, 1957.

Immergluck, L. Determinism-freedom in contemporary psychology: an ancient problem revisited. *American Psychologist,* 1964, 19, 270–281.

Jackson, B. White-collar pill party. *Atlantic Monthly,* 1966, August, 35–40.

James, W. *Will to believe.* New York: Longmans, 1896.

Jarvik, M. The psychopharmacological revolution. *Psychology Today,* 1967, 1, 51–59.

Josephson, E., & Josephson, M. (Eds.), *Man alone.* New York: Dell, 1962.

Kahn, H., & Wiener, A. *The year 2000.* New York: Macmillan, 1967.

Kamiya, J. Conscious control of brain waves. *Psychology Today,* 1968, 11, 57–60.

Karlins, M. Conceptual complexity and remote-associative proficiency as creativity variables in a complex problem-solving task. *Journal of Personality and Social Psychology,* 1967, 6, 264–278.

Karlins, M. Some empirical support for an exploration stage in the creative process. *Journal of Creative Behavior,* 1968, 2, 256–262.

Karlins, M. *The last man is out.* Englewood Cliffs, N.J.: Prentice-Hall, 1969.

Karlins, M., & Abelson, H. *Persuasion.* New York: Springer, 1970.

Kelly, G. *The psychology of personal constructs,* Vol. I. New York: Norton, 1955.

Keniston, K. *The uncommitted.* New York: Harcourt, 1960.

Keniston, K. *Young radicals.* New York: Harcourt, 1968.

Kneller, G. *Existentialism and education.* New York: Philosophical Library, 1958.

Koch, S. Psychological science versus the science-humanism antinomy: Intimations of a significant science of man. *American Psychologist,* 1961, **16,** 629–639.

Koestler, A. *The act of creation.* New York: Macmillan, 1964.

Koestler, A. *Ghost in the machine.* New York: Macmillan, 1967.

Krasner, L. Behavior control and social responsibility. *American Psychologist,* 1962, **17,** 199–204.

Krutch, J. *The measure of man.* New York: Bobbs-Merrill, 1954.

Kuhn, T. *The structure of scientific revolutions.* Chicago: University of Chicago Press, 1962.

Kurtz, P. *Decision and the condition of man.* Seattle: University of Washington Press, 1965.

Kurtz, P. The individual, the organization, and participatory democracy. In P. Kurtz (Ed.), *Moral problems in contemporary society.* Englewood Cliffs, N.J.: Prentice-Hall, 1969. Pp. 189–209.

Lashley, K. The problem of serial order in the brain. In L. Jeffress (Ed.), *Cerebral mechanisms in behavior.* New York: Wiley, 1951. Pp. 112–135.

Lederberg, J. Experimental genetics and human evolution. *Bulletin of the Atomic Scientists,* 1966, **22,** 4–11.

Lent, J. Mimosa cottage: Experiment in hope. *Psychology Today,* 1968, **2,** 51–58.

Levine, S., & Conner, R. Endocrine aspects of violence. An unpublished staff report to the National Commission on the Causes and Prevention of Violence, December, 1969.

London, P. *Behavior control.* New York: Harper & Row, 1969.

Lovejoy, A. The paradox of the thinking behaviorist. *Philadelphia Review,* 1922, **31,** 135–147.

Luria, S. Directed genetic change. In T. M. Sonneborn (Ed.), *The control of human heredity and evolution*. New York: Macmillan, 1965. Pp. 1–19.

Lynd, R. *Knowledge for what?* Princeton, N.J.: Princeton University Press, 1939.

MacKay, D. Conscious control of the brain. In J. Eccles (Ed.), *Brain and conscious experience*. New York: Springer-Verlag, 1966.

Maddi, S. The existential neurosis. *Journal of Abnormal Psychology*, 1967, **72**, 311–325.

Mann, J. *Changing human behavior*. New York: Scribner, 1965.

Marcson, S. (Ed.) *Automation, alienation, and anomie*. New York: Harper & Row, 1970.

Marcuse, H. *One-dimensional man*. Boston: Beacon, 1964.

Maslow, A. *Toward a psychology of being*. Princeton, N.J.: Van Nostrand, 1962.

Maslow, A. *The psychology of science*. New York: Harper & Row, 1966.

May, R. *Man's search for himself*. New York: Norton, 1953.

May, R. *Psychology and the human dilemma*. Princeton, N.J.: Van Nostrand, 1967.

May, R. *Love and will*. New York: Norton, 1969.

McCain, G., & Segal, E. *The game of science*. Belmont, Calif.: Wadsworth, 1969.

Merton, R. *Social theory and social structure*. New York: Free Press, 1949.

Miller, G. A. On turning psychology over to the unwashed. *Psychology Today*, 1969, **3**, December, 53–54, 66–74.

Mills, C. W. *The sociological imagination*. New York: Oxford, 1959.

Muller, H. Means and aims in human genetic betterment. In T. M. Sonneborn (Ed.), *The control of human heredity and evolution*. New York: Macmillan, 1965. Pp. 100–122.

Muller, H. What genetic course will man steer? *Bulletin of the Atomic Scientists*, 1968, 24, 6–12.

Nagel, E. *The structure of science*. New York: Harcourt, 1961.

New York Times editorial. Push-button people. April 10, 1967, p. 34.

New York Times editorial. Brainwave? September 19, 1970, p. 28.

Nisbet, R. *The quest for community*. New York: Oxford, 1953.

Olds, J. The central nervous system and the reinforcement of behavior. *American Psychologist*, 1969, **24**, 114–132.

Olds, J., & Milner, P. Positive reinforcement produced by electrical stimulation of septal area and other regions of rat brain. *Journal of Comparative and Physiological Psychology*, 1954, **47**, 419–427.

Oppenheimer, J. R. Analogy in science. *American Psychologist*, 1956, **11**, 127–135.

Orwell, G. *1984*. New York: Harcourt, 1949.

Penfield, W. The interpretive cortex. *Science*, 1959, **129**, 1719–1725.

Perls, F., Hefferline, R., & Goodman, P. *Gestalt therapy*. New York: Dell, 1951.

Platt, J. R. *The step to man*. New York: Wiley, 1966.

Popper, K. *The open society and its enemies*, Vol. I. Princeton, N.J.: Princeton University Press, 1950.

Quarton, G. Deliberate efforts to control human behavior and modify personality. *Daedalus*, 1967, **96**, 837–853.

Riesman, D. *The lonely crowd*. New Haven: Yale University Press, 1950.

Riesman, D., & Harris, T. G. The young are captives of each other: a conversation with David Riesman. *Psychology Today*, 1969, **3**, 28–31, 63–67

Roe, A. Man's forgotten weapon. *American Psychologist*, 1959, **14**, 261–266.

Rogers, C. Cultural evolution as viewed by psychologists. *Daedalus*, 1961, **90**, 574–575.

Rogers, C., & Skinner, B. Some issues concerning the control of human behavior: A symposium. *Science*, 1956, **124**, 1057–1066.

Rogow, A. *The psychiatrists*. New York: Putnam, 1970.

Rosenfeld, A. *Second genesis*. New York: Prentice-Hall, 1969.

Rostand, J. *Can man be modified?* New York: Basic Books, 1959.

Roszak, T. *The making of a counter culture*. New York: Doubleday, 1969.

Russell, B. *Our knowledge of the external world*. New York: Norton, 1929.

Ryle, G. *The concept of mind*. New York: Barnes and Noble, 1949.

Saunders, J. Introduction. In S. M. Farber and R. M. Wilson (Eds.). *The control of the mind*. New York: McGraw-Hill, 1961.

Schein, E. The Chinese indoctrination program for prisoners of war. *Psychiatry*, 1956, **19**, 149–172.

Schroder, H., Driver, M., & Streufert, S. *Human information processing*. New York: Holt, Rinehart and Winston, 1967.

Schroder, H., Karlins, M., & Phares, J. *Teaching children to be free.* Prepublication manuscript, 1971.

Seidel, G. *The crisis of creativity.* Notre Dame, Ind.: University of Notre Dame Press, 1966.

Shick, A. The cybernetic state. *Transaction,* 1970, **7**, 14–26.

Skinner, B. *Walden two.* New York: Macmillan, 1948.

Skinner, B. *Science and human behavior.* New York: Macmillan, 1953.

Skinner, B. Freedom and the control of men. *The American Scholar,* 1955–1956, **25**, 47–65.

Skinner, B. *Verbal behavior.* New York: Appleton-Century-Crofts, 1957.

Skinner, B. Contingencies of reinforcement in the design of a culture. *Behavioral Science,* 1966, **11**, 159–166.

Sonneborn, T. *Control of human heredity and evolution.* New York: Macmillan, 1965.

Sperry, R. Mind, brain, and humanist values. In J. Platt (Ed.), *New views of the nature of man.* Chicago: University of Chicago Press, 1965. Pp. 71–92.

Sykes, G. (Ed.). *Alienation: The cultural climate of our time.* New York: Braziller, 1964.

Tart, C. (Ed.) *States of altered consciousness.* New York: Wiley, 1969.

Taylor, G. *The passages of thought.* New York: Oxford University Press, 1969.

Taylor, Gordon R. *The biological time bomb.* New York: World, 1968.

Toennies, F. *Fundamental concepts of sociology* (C. P. Loomis, Trans.). New York: American Book, 1940.

Toffler, A. *Future shock.* New York: Random House, 1970.

Tolman, E. Cognitive maps in rats and men. *Psychological Review,* 1948, **55**, 189–208.

Townsend, R. *Up the organization.* New York: Knopf, 1970.

Ulrich, R., Stachnik, T., & Mabry, J. (Eds.) *Control of human behavior.* Glenview, Ill.: Scott, Foresman, 1966.

Wald, G. Determinancy, individuality, and the problem of free will. In J. Platt (Ed.), *New views of the nature of man.* Chicago: University of Chicago Press, 1965. Pp. 16–46.

Watson, J. Psychology as the behaviorist views it. *Psychological Review,* 1913, **20,** 158–177.

Watson, J. *Behaviorism.* Chicago: University of Chicago Press, 1924.

Watson, J., & Rayner, R. Conditioned emotional reactions. *Journal of Experimental Psychology,* 1920, **3,** 1–14.

Wheelis, A. *The quest for identity.* New York: Norton, 1958.

White, W. *Beyond conformity.* New York: Free Press, 1961.

Whorf, B. *Language, thought, and reality.* Cambridge, Mass.: M.I.T. Press, 1956.

Yablonsky, L. *The hippie trip.* New York: Pegasus, 1968.

# Annotated List
# of Suggested Readings

## Chapter 1: Brave New Behavior Control: The Final Revolution?

Davison, G. Elimination of a sadistic fantasy by a client-controlled counter-conditioning technique. *Journal of Abnormal Psychology*, 1968, **73**, 84–90. Behavior modification is used to treat a young man with an unwanted sexual fantasy.

Delgado, J. *Physical control of the mind*. New York: Harper & Row, 1969. A world-renowned scientist-surgeon presents a fascinating account of his (and others') efforts to control animal and human behavior through electrical stimulation of the brain.

Heath, R. Electrical self-stimulation of the brain in man. *American Journal of Psychiatry*, 1963, **120**, 571–577. Interesting case studies of two patients undergoing electrical stimulation of the brain.

Jarvik, M. The psychopharmacological revolution. *Psychology Today*, 1967, **1**, 51–59. A clearly written analysis of the new drugs in our drug-oriented society.

Karlins, M. *The last man is out.* Englewood Cliffs, N.J.: Prentice-Hall, 1969. Behavior modification principles are combined with computer technology to direct the destiny of a major league baseball team.

London, P. *Behavior control.* New York: Harper & Row, 1969. A sound, elaborate examination of modern behavior control procedures.

Penfield, W. The interpretive cortex. *Science,* 1959, **129,** 1719–1725. Patients vividly recall memories while undergoing brain stimulation.

Skinner, B. Contingencies of reinforcement in the design of a culture. *Behavioral Science,* 1966, **11,** 159–166. One of America's leading scientists presents a psychological procedure for overcoming three contemporary social problems: excessive eating, excessive procreation, and excessive pugnacity.

Sonneborn, T. (Ed.) *The control of human heredity and evolution.* New York: Macmillan, 1965. Five papers by five leading scientists on genetic engineering. Particularly interesting is Muller's "Means and Aims in Human Genetic Betterment."

Ulrich, R., Stachnik, T., & Mabry, J. (Eds.) *Control of human behavior.* Glenview, Ill.: Scott, Foresman, 1966. A collection of studies describing attempts to regulate human behavior, mostly through operant conditioning procedures developed by B. F. Skinner. Included are the researches of Watson and Rayner and of Fuller.

## Chapter 2: Living with the Faustian Power

Amis, K. *New maps of hell.* New York: Harcourt, 1960. A splendid and thorough review of modern science fiction literature with sections on behavior control stories.

Becker, E. *The structure of evil.* New York: Braziller, 1968. A history of intellectual thought on the application of social science.

Huxley, A. *Island.* New York: Harper & Row, 1962. An interesting contrast to Huxley's most famous novel, *Brave New World,* in that it demonstrates how behavior control techniques can be used to create a better society.

Jackson, B. White-collar pill party. *Atlantic Monthly,* 1966, August, 35–40. A well-written account of "mature" adults who are already abusing mind drugs.

Kahn, H., & Wiener, A. *The year 2000.* New York: Macmillan, 1967.

Karlins, M., & Abelson, H. *Persuasion.* New York: Springer, 1970. A discussion of the factors that lead people to change their attitudes and opinions. Advances in the scientific study of persuasion are highlighted.

Koestler, A. *The ghost in the machine.* New York: Macmillan, 1967. Contains a fanciful, but interesting, argument in favor of redesigning all human brains with chemicals.

Krasner, L. Behavior control and social responsibility. *American Psychologist,* 1962, **17,** 199–204.

Rogers, C., & Skinner, B. Some issues concerning the control of human behavior. *Science,* 1956, **124,** 1057–1066.

Skinner, B. *Science and human behavior.* New York: Macmillan, 1953. Describes in detail the implications of behavioral science for human affairs.

## Chapter 3: Two Visions

Bennis, W., & Harris, T. G. Warren Bennis, a conversation. *Psychology Today,* 1970, February, 48–54+. An optimistic discussion of future social organization.

Ellul, J. *The technological society.* New York: Knopf, 1964. A far-ranging inquiry into the nature of organizational democracy.

Fromm, E. *Revolution of hope.* New York: Harper & Row, 1968. A proposal for creating a participatory democracy.

Galbraith, J. *The new industrial state.* Boston: Houghton Mifflin, 1967. On the economics of organizational democracy.

Huxley, A. *Brave new world.* New York: Doubleday, 1932. Still the best fictionalized projection of a psytocracy.

Keniston, K. *Young radicals.* New York: Harcourt, 1968. Elaborates on the psychological antecedents of youthful dissent against the current technological order.

Kurtz, P. The individual, the organization, and participatory democracy. In P. Kurtz (Ed.) *Moral problems in contemporary society*. New York: Prentice-Hall, 1969.

Shick, A. The cybernetic state. *Transaction,* 1970, February, 14–26. Discusses the potential of technology to produce either a psytocracy or a participatory democracy.

## Chapter 4: Reflections on the American Character While Standing in a New York Subway Station

Burrows, D., & Lapides, F. (Eds.) *Alienation: A casebook.* New York: Crowell, 1969. A collection of works on alienation by leading scholars and writers.

Keniston, K. *The uncommitted.* New York: Harcourt, 1960. An in-depth study of alienated youth in America.

Marcuse, H. *One-dimensional man.* Boston: Beacon, 1964. A philosopher of the Left examines some of the causes of contemporary alienation. Difficult reading.

May, R. *Love and will.* New York: Norton, 1969. Man's current state of alienation is powerfully described and analyzed in this major work.

Seeman, M. On the meaning of alienation. *American Sociological Review,* 1959, 24, 783–791. A good discussion of the five meanings of alienation: powerlessness, meaninglessness, normlessness, isolation, and self-estrangement.

## Chapter 5: The Alienated American and the Specter of Psytocracy

Fromm, E. *Escape from freedom.* New York: Holt, Rinehart and Winston, 1941. A brilliant psychological examination of the factors underlying modern man's flight from freedom.

McCain, G., & Segal, E. *The game of science.* Belmont, Calif.: Wadsworth, 1969.

## Chapter 6: Putting Man Down and Building Man Up

Branden, N. *The psychology of self-esteem.* Los Angeles: Nash Publishing Company, 1969.

Diggory, J. *Self-evaluation: Concepts and studies.* New York: Wiley, 1966.

Fromm, E. *The sane society.* New York: Holt, Rinehart and Winston, 1955. An investigation into the manipulation of modern man through the systematic attack on his self-concept.

Immergluck, L. Determinism-freedom in contemporary psychology: An ancient problem revisited. *American Psychologist,* 1964, **19,** 270–281. A refutation of various arguments for freedom.

Koestler, A. *The act of creation.* New York: Macmillan, 1964. Contains an overzealous, but well-written, history of antimentalism in behavioral science.

Maslow, A. *The psychology of science.* New York: Harper & Row, 1966. A clinical psychologist's appraisal of reductionist tendencies in behavioral science.

*Psychology Today,* April 1969. The entire issue is dedicated to a discussion of mechanical man.

Roszak, T. *The making of a counter culture.* New York: Doubleday, 1969. Typifies the antiscience reaction to the vision of mechanical man.

## Chapter 7: A Future for Freedom?

Bruner, J. *Towards a theory of instruction.* Cambridge, Mass.: Harvard University Press, 1966. Advocates the application of process psychology principles to education.

Chomsky, N. *Language and mind.* New York: Harcourt, 1968. An excellent summary of linguistic arguments for process psychology.

Miller, G. The magical number seven, plus or minus two: Some limits on our capacity for information processing. *Psychological Review,* 1956, **63,** 81–96.

Platt, J. *The step to man.* New York: Wiley, 1966.

Schroder, H., Driver, M., & Streufert, S. *Human information processing.* New York: Holt, Rinehart & Winston, 1967. A compendium of studies and experiments in process psychology.

Sperry, R. Mind, brain and human values. In J. Platt (Ed.), *New views of the nature of man.* Chicago: University of Chicago Press, 1965. An argument for human freedom within the context of scientific determinism.

Tolman, E. Cognitive maps in rats and men. *Psychological Review,* 1948, **55**, 189–208. The precursor of process psychology.